Praise for *Healthy Leadership*

"*Healthy Leadership* perfectly captures the leader of the future, and how you can become the executive your team and company need. Filled with practical and actionable tools to get started with today, this book will revolutionize your work, career, and life!"

Dr. Marshall Goldsmith

Thinkers50 #1 Executive Coach and New York Times best-selling author of *Triggers, Mojo,* and *What Got You Here Won't Get You There*

"The principles and practices of *Healthy Leadership* come down to a simple truth I've been talking about for years: It's not about you—it's about the people you serve. Lee and Julie have created a hands-on guidebook to help you become the kind of leader people are searching for right now. If you believe Healthy Leadership matters in today's workplace, read this book!"

Ken Blanchard

Coauthor of *The New One Minute Manager* and *Simple Truths of Leadership*

"At Edward Jones, we ask our associates to lead with courage in ways that are purpose-driven and leader-led. *Healthy Leadership* is about what it takes to help high-performing teams feel supported and succeed in serving their clients, colleagues, and communities. It's how to lead with purpose."

Penny Pennington

Managing Partner, Edward Jones

"*Healthy Leadership* is like Google maps for today's leader. It's a trusted guide for leading in a new world of work. The starting point is where you are today. The destination is a win for everyone involved – the leader, the team, and the business."

Daniel L. Jones

Chairman & CEO, Encore Wire

"Lee and Julie's insights are always so valuable due to extensive research and work with companies of all sizes. Applying the concepts and tools from *Healthy Leadership* will help your company cement a healthy culture that will make your team members stay and thrive."

Valerie Freeman
CEO, Imprimis Group, Inc.

"The world of work has clearly changed. This excellent book is a practical guide for leaders who want to thrive in this new world, to be a positive force for good. *Healthy leadership* will change your business!"

Frank Dulcich
Chairman & CEO, Pacific Seafood Group

"In *Healthy Leadership*, Lee and Julie emphasize how healthy leadership is about healthy relationships with everyone we interact with in life. We must invest in our relationships and should celebrate them along the way. Well worth investing your time reading their new book! There are many concepts for you to apply in your daily life."

Bill Dyer
CEO, Standard Nutrition

"Lee and Julie are dynamic and visionary thought leaders. More importantly, they have hearts for helping others succeed and making meaningful contributions while leading significant lives. Their new book, *Healthy Leadership*, creates a real synergy with people, the organizations they choose to work for, and then decide to stay and grow with."

Denis G. Simon
Senior Executive Vice President, Challenger, Gray & Christmas, Inc.

"*Healthy Leadership* concisely outlines the mindset and actions for successful leadership of today's workforce. The authors' unique combination of practical science, engaging stories, and proven tools equips the reader to elevate his/her leadership game."

Jeanne Mason
Sr. Vice President, Human Resources, Baxter International Inc.

"In applying the concept of health to leadership, Lee and Julie provide a powerful framework for growth at every level. *Healthy Leadership* provides a powerful reminder to the enduring power of love, positivity, growth, clarity, connection, and coaching."

Raanan Horowitz
President and CEO, Elbit America

"*Healthy Leadership* is the most deliberate and practical book I have read on the contemporary requirements for being an impactful leader. It will help leaders and organizations grow and compete in the future. Most writings on this subject are long and theoretical, but this book is concise and gets right to the point on how to be a healthy leader."

Dave Loeser
Founder, FutureSolve

"*Healthy Leadership* is an excellent read for leaders who desire to lead with purpose. It's filled with practical tools to help leaders empower their teams to experience monumental professional growth and give their best work back to the organization. Applying its principles and practices will make your organization a sought-after place for people to work and thrive."

Sarah Shadonix
Founder and CEO, Scout & Cellar

"*Healthy Leadership* is a timely guide that equips leaders to elevate others. That starts with healthy principles that fulfill the needs of today's worker and practices that engage and encourage people. This book helps leaders transform themselves, their teams, and their organizations."

Paul R. Hays
CEO, Med-Pharmex, Inc.

"In a world where distancing has become the norm, *Healthy Leadership* brings back the importance of human connection to drive successful leadership. It's a practical guide that equips leaders with the emotional skills to engage, encourage, and motivate their teams. *Healthy Leadership* is a wonderful addition to my collection of the Colans' books."

Thomas Vanderheyden
Vice President, Global Sales, Advanced Energy Industries, Inc.

Additional Titles by the Authors

The Power of Positive Coaching

The 5 Coaching Habits of Excellent Leaders

Stick with It: Mastering the Art of Adherence

Engaging the Hearts and Minds of All Your Employees

Orchestrating Attitude: Getting the Best from Yourself and Others

7 Moments . . . That Define Excellent Leaders

Leadership Matters: Daily Insights to Inspire Extraordinary Results

Power Exchange:
Boosting Accountability and Performance in Today's Workforce

107 Ways to Stick to It:
Practical Tips to Achieve the Success You Deserve

Inspire! Connecting with Students to Make a Difference

The Nature of Excellence

Winners Always Quit:
Seven Pretty Good Habits You Can Swap for Really Great Results

Getting the BEST from Yourself and Others

Passionate Performance:
Engaging Hearts and Minds to Conquer the Competition

Sticking to It: The Art of Adherence

HEALTHY
LEADERSHIP

How to Thrive
in the New World of Work

an actionable guide for leaders

From the best-selling authors of
Sticking to It: Mastering the Art of Adherence

Lee J. Colan
Julie Davis-Colan

Healthy Leadership

How to Thrive in the New World of Work

International rights and foreign translations available only through negotiation with CornerStone Leadership Institute.

Inquiries regarding permission for use of the material contained in this book should be addressed to:

CornerStone Leadership Institute
P.O. Box 764087
Dallas, TX 75376
972-298-8377

ISBN: 978-0-9600155-4-2

Printed in the United States of America.

Developmental Editor: Aaron Shulman, amshulman@gmail.com
Copy Editor: Deb Johnson, dj@spikecommunications.com
Proofreader: Kathleen Green Pothier, kg@positivelyproofed.com
Cover and Interior Design: Melissa Farr, melissa@backporchcreative.com

CornerStone
Leadership Institute

To our children, Cameron, Grace, and Lexi.

May you become healthy leaders and inspire future healthy leaders.

Table of Contents

1

Leading in Today's World of Work

Something is healthy when it is in an optimal state of well-being. We strive for healthy relationships, a healthy diet, a healthy body, a healthy mind, healthy emotions, healthy perspectives, healthy conversation, healthy awareness, and healthy finances. With all this focus on healthy everything, we asked, "What about healthy leadership?" There are far too many examples of destructive, *un*healthy leadership. Yet in today's world of work, if you want to be competitive, understanding and applying the principles and practices of healthy leadership is key.

Healthy leadership focuses on the health and growth of all parties: the leader, the team, and the business.

If the team thrives, so does the business and everyone it serves. In other words, healthy leadership drives healthy growth for all stakeholders. Cultivating healthy leadership is not automatic. It doesn't just happen on its own. It is a *choice*. If you choose to apply the actionable strategies and tools we share in the pages ahead, you will predictably reap rewards that include:

- A purpose-driven organization and team members;

- A culture that is safe and innovative and makes team members want to stay;

- Intellectually and emotionally engaged teams;

- Team members working in their gifted areas who flourish;

- Excellent execution that drives healthy results.

Healthy leadership matters because unusually high-performing teams are the ultimate advantage for any organization—a business, a nonprofit, a sports team, or a family for that matter. In today's ultra-competitive marketplace, good results just aren't good enough. Innovative or unique products or services might get you into the game, but only your team can create a "wall" that is too high and difficult for your competitors to climb. To win, you need to produce extraordinary results, which only come from extraordinary teams. And where there is an extraordinary team, you can bet there is a healthy leader. That's why leadership—specifically, *your* leadership—matters.

Research bears this out. In fact, according to one study, up to 70 percent of variance in an organization's performance is attributable to leadership behavior.[1] Nothing has a bigger impact on organizational success than leadership—not culture, strategy, processes, or incentive systems.[2] The single most important factor influencing the growth of your company is *how you lead.*

Grow yourself, grow your people, grow your business.

Leadership as a Leading Indicator

Consider a measurement continuum. At one end are *lagging indicators.* These are the results of your team's past performance. They enable you to see if your activities produced the desired outcomes. At the other end of the continuum are *leading indicators.* These are the drivers of your team's future performance. They provide early warning signs of problems that might appear on the horizon. This continuum illustrates how leadership acts as the most crucial leading indicator of sustained, healthy growth:

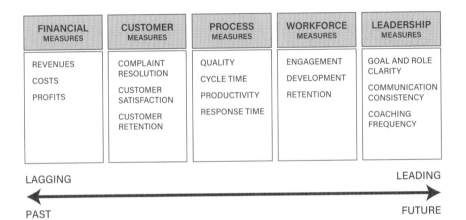

FINANCIAL MEASURES	CUSTOMER MEASURES	PROCESS MEASURES	WORKFORCE MEASURES	LEADERSHIP MEASURES
REVENUES COSTS PROFITS	COMPLAINT RESOLUTION CUSTOMER SATISFACTION CUSTOMER RETENTION	QUALITY CYCLE TIME PRODUCTIVITY RESPONSE TIME	ENGAGEMENT DEVELOPMENT RETENTION	GOAL AND ROLE CLARITY COMMUNICATION CONSISTENCY COACHING FREQUENCY

LAGGING   LEADING

PAST   FUTURE

Economic and competitive pressures compel many leaders to focus on lagging indicators, typically financial ones. Of course, it's important to consider lagging indicators to know how well you have performed in the past. However, you must be careful not to neglect leading indicators, since you want to be able to predict how your organization will perform six, nine, or twelve months from now. A singular focus on lagging indicators gives you little opportunity for corrective action if your team drifts off course. Healthy leaders look at both lagging and leading indicators, which allows them to connect the past and the future and to paint a more complete picture of team health.

Today's Employee Priorities

Healthy leadership is more vital today than ever because peoples' relationship to work has changed, and so has the nature of work itself. Expansive research by Gallup clearly shows that today's worker is more purpose-driven, development-oriented, and focused on strengths.[3]

Purpose over paycheck. Your team members don't just work for a paycheck—they want meaning. They want to work for organizations with a compelling purpose. Compensation is important and must be fair, but it's rarely the sole driver of career choices. And Ping-Pong tables, cappuccino machines, free snacks, and such are not strong motivators, either. The emphasis for today's team member has switched from paycheck to purpose, and so must your leadership approach.

Development over satisfaction. Today's employees are not pursuing mere job satisfaction. They strive for development—both personal and professional, which are increasingly inseparable. They want self-growth and a position in an enterprise that is itself growing—so that they can contribute to it and be part of its story. As a result, they don't want bosses. They want *coaches.* They want someone in their corner who values them as both a person and an employee—someone who helps them understand and cultivate their strengths.

Strengths over weaknesses. Today's team members don't want to focus on fixing their weaknesses; rather, they want your help in building their strengths. Weaknesses rarely, if ever, transform into strengths, while strengths can develop infinitely. Leaders should not ignore weaknesses but instead put employees in positions to maximize strengths. This benefits both the individual and the organization.

This new healthy leadership model benefits leaders at every level, and everyone they work with. It matters in an up economy or a down economy, in a start-up or a mature business, a local company or a global enterprise. It matters when you are in the boardroom and when you are in the break room. Leadership matters . . . and healthy leadership inspires everyone to thrive.

To win in the marketplace, you must first win in the workplace.

—DOUG CONANT,
former CEO, Campbell Soup Company,
and former Chairman, Avon Products

Principles and Practices

Healthy leadership addresses human needs—it's personal. This new approach to leadership is comprised of three principles and three practices that are no longer just nice to do in today's new world of work. Healthy leadership is like a cultural magnet that attracts people to your team and the cultural glue that makes them want to stay. If today's workers don't see healthy leadership, they will look for it elsewhere.

Healthy leadership is not about the leader, but it starts with the leader. It's about the people you serve. As a leader, when you help others grow, you grow—and growing people fuel growing, healthy organizations. The healthy leader's success is measured in what others achieve—the leader's impact is multiplied through others.

The three healthy leadership principles and definitions are:

Love: Do what is in the best interest of others.

Positivity: Manage negative emotions and increase positive ones.

Growth: Seek new insights, knowledge, and skills.

The three healthy leadership practices and definitions are:

Clarify: Crystalize a desired future and motivation to get there.

Connect: Build ties between work and human needs.

Coach: Unlock the potential in others.

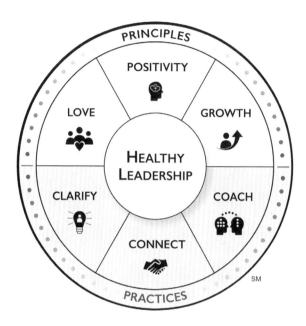

The three healthy leadership principles are like an operating system. In fact, let's call them *PrinciplesOS*. This operating system supports the "apps" of healthy leadership—the practices. Your ability to implement the principles of love, positivity, and growth will either enhance or inhibit the effectiveness of your apps—healthy leadership practices of clarify, connect, and coach. The alignment between principles and practices is key, particularly with today's worker, who deeply values authenticity and integrity.

In our work with clients for over 23 years, we have witnessed firsthand how these principles and practices enable leaders to inspire growth for all parties in our new, rapidly evolving world of work. Principles and practices that distinguished great leaders yesterday are basic requirements today. Challenges around sustained remote work and employees' desire to see the human behind the leader are forcing leaders to elevate their games to be more human, more connected, clearer, and more positive.

In this actionable guide, we will share the art and science of healthy leadership. The art comes into play in how you choose to authentically adapt these tools to your unique style and your team's unique needs. The science comes into play by understanding universal human dynamics and insights about behavior and how our brains work, then applying proven tools to get the best from yourself and those you are leading.

Healthy leadership is a process, not an event. To get in good physical shape, you must exercise each day, but you don't exactly know when you'll see results. You must trust the process. Let's start working your leadership muscle and address the three healthy leadership principles and practices to help you and your team thrive.

You can have everything in life you want,
if you will help enough other people get what they want.
—ZIG ZIGLAR,
American author and motivational speaker

HEALTHY LEADERSHIP
PRINCIPLES

LOVE

Do what is in the best interest of others

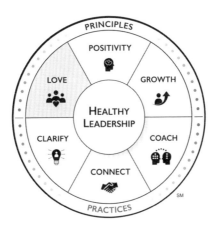

December 15, 2020, started out like any other day for Anthony Gaskin. He woke up, put on his brown UPS uniform, hopped into his delivery truck, and set off to make the day's rounds dropping off packages on his route in Chester County, Virginia. But something odd happened as he pulled into the neighborhood where he often delivered over 180 packages a day. Families and cars were gathered along the sides of the road as though the people were waiting for a parade to pass by. Stranger still, many of them held up signs, and the signs said things like, "We love Anthony!" and "Thank you for your kindness!" As he drove past the crowds, they cheered, clapped, and honked their horns at him. What the heck was going on?

It turned out that the neighborhood on Anthony's delivery route had decided to come out in force to demonstrate how much they appreciated him. Throughout the pandemic, he had been a consistently uplifting presence in their lives. He always waved from his truck and brought a needed ray of light into their days with his smile and conversation. And he maintained this upbeat attitude even as the volume of packages increased dramatically due to a spike in home deliveries and the holiday season, saddling him with an even heavier workload. So, one neighbor took it upon herself to rally others to show him how grateful they were.

"I was in shock," Anthony said. "My heart was overjoyed."[1]

What we find emotional about this story isn't just the well-deserved outpouring of appreciation Anthony received, though that is inspiring. There is also a bigger, less obvious lesson in what this community did.

As the sign stated, the people of the neighborhood loved Anthony. Yet we rarely publicly express feelings of love except with our close family and friends, and even with these loved ones it can sometimes be hard to find the right words. But the people on Anthony's route understood that an expression of love in a context in which love is rarely expressed—between a UPS driver and his customers—would have a profound effect. And it did. Anthony was brought to tears by learning what he meant to the community, and the story of what had happened ended up on the national news, touching peoples' hearts across the country. Once you let love break out of its customary box, it can bring new warmth and depth to our lives. In particular, love can yield powerful outcomes in the world of work. But it shouldn't be reserved exclusively for exceptional gestures like the one that occurred in Chester County. It should be part of the fabric of everyday life at work and at home.

Love and Leadership

Love is the source of most everything that is good and healthy . . . at home and at work. It is the most talked about, written about, and sung about topic in the world. You certainly always love your children even though you might not always like their actions or attitudes. The same is true for healthy leaders. They love their people even though they might not always like or agree with their actions or attitudes. So, love is the first of the three principles of healthy leadership. Indeed, it has been embedded in more businesses than you might initially think.

Whole Foods co-founder John Mackey dedicates a whole chapter to love in his book, *Conscious Capitalism*. Southwest Airlines, whose NYSE ticker code is LUV, makes frequent and explicit reference to its corporate culture of love. Author Ken Blanchard and Colleen Barrett, president emeritus of Southwest Airlines, even co-authored a book titled *Lead with LUV*. They are not the only business thought leaders to articulate the importance of love in high-performing organizations. In *The Leadership Challenge* by James Kouzes and Barry Posner, a widely read and applied leadership book, the authors conclude that love is the "best kept secret" of exemplary leaders. More recently, Marcus Buckingham, known for his data-driven writing, wrote *Love + Work* where he takes a more human stance. He argues how work today is intensely personal and that we need to feel fully seen and heard. In other words, today's worker wants to feel loved at work.

Additionally, PepsiCo, Southwest Airlines, The Container Store, and Zappos all list "love" or "caring" among their corporate values. Scientific research has even yielded clear evidence of the practical benefits of bringing love into business. Management professors Sigal Barsade and Olivia O'Neill have shown that workplace cultures of love are correlated with increased levels of teamwork, job satisfaction, and improved customer outcomes.[2]

Love is an indispensable principle of healthy leadership, but for it to have an impact on your team, it must be more than just a noun—it must also be a verb. This means that healthy leaders *act* on love more than they talk about it. As Colleen Barrett puts it, "What's important is the fact that you're honoring people and acknowledging that what they do makes a positive difference. In the process, you are making heroes out of them. You are letting them know that you love them for their efforts, and you want everybody to celebrate their success."[3]

This is what the people on Anthony Gaskin's delivery route did for him; moreover, they did so at an especially poignant moment, during the stressful flurry of the holiday season after an already stressful year. Customers showed their love for Anthony; they let him know he was a hero. We need more of this spirit, not only from customers to service providers, but also among leaders and their teams.

Healthy relationships are the foundation of healthy leadership, and healthy relationships are grounded in love. This begs the question of what, exactly, we mean by love in today's world of work. To provide an answer, let's look at how you can bring the principle of love to life within your team.

What's love got to do with it? . . . Everything!

Put the Team Before Me

Healthy leaders choose to meet the needs of their teams first. When leading with love, the needs of others come before our own, and the team's health and success are a healthy leader's true measure of success. It reminds us of our son's former high school football coach, Chris Cunningham, who preached this same leadership concept of "team over me." He even had T-shirts printed with a BIG "team" and a little tiny "me":

TEAM

me

For a healthy leader, your feelings must be subordinated to the demands of a higher cause: serving your employees.

Putting your team first to lead with love requires a crucial quality: humility. British writer C.S. Lewis described humility well when he wrote that it "is not thinking less of yourself, but thinking of yourself less." Healthy leadership, likewise, is about focusing on other people—not on yourself. This is especially relevant when your team brings home a big win, since success tempts even the humblest person among us to sing our own praises. But you must genuinely credit others' contributions above all else. Humility is also the seed of continuous learning, an idea we will address further in the chapter on Growth.

A few years ago, Lee had the privilege of interviewing Colleen Barrett, who has since become a dear friend. As we mentioned, she is president emeritus at Southwest Airlines, and she has been the chief nurturer of the company's famously positive culture. Colleen is a paragon of humility. She likes to say she is a better follower than she is a leader.[4] During her conversation with Lee, she discussed the concept of "followership," arguing that following can be just as important as leading when it comes to creating a thriving company. You, as a leader, likely won't be a specialist in all the areas your team relies on, which is why you hire people who specialize in those roles. Naturally, then, it follows that you will be listening to experts most of the time rather than talking as one yourself. An important part of a healthy leader's job is to listen to and follow the people on his/her team.

Leading with love is simply doing what is in the best interest of others, and this requires humility. Now let's examine ways you can bring other aspects of love to life within your team.

If you honor and serve the people who work for you, they will honor and serve you.

—MARY KAY ASH,
founder of Mary Kay Cosmetics

Be Human

Most of us have a moment in childhood when we realize that our parents are not superheroes. Then, when we're a little older, we realize that not only are they not superheroes, they're in fact imperfect, often feel vulnerable, and occasionally even have no idea what the best course of action is. In other words, they are just like us. This can be a confusing transition at first, but as you grow into adulthood, you get used to seeing your parents as humans. This can even become comforting, offering a new way to connect with them and learn. And yet, when we mature into leaders in our professional lives, we often fall into a pattern that echoes that experience of being a kid—we think we must come off to our team as a confident, infallible person with all the answers. But this is the wrong approach. Healthy leaders know how to lead without constructing a façade of total control.

Employees are yearning for a more human connection with their leaders. They don't want parent-like figures who appear to have all the answers (but, of course, don't have all of them). They want leaders who are courageous enough to be human—to be real and transparent—and build genuine connections and credible reputations with their teams. And credibility comes from being open with your team about challenges and uncertainty—and about the fact that you make the best decision you can today, but you might change your mind tomorrow with new information. This humanizes you in your team's eyes, helping them to see you're a person just like them, trying to navigate obstacles as best you can. Additionally, you're more likely to inspire employees to collaborate and offer ideas that they would have kept silent about if you had acted all-knowing. We're not suggesting you voice every insecurity, concern, or point of confusion. Your team needs to trust in your ability to steer the ship through the rocky waters of change and uncertainty. But a healthy leader knows that showing your humanity is not a liability. Instead, it offers an often-overlooked advantage.

See the Human Behind the Employee

It is important to be human with your team, but it is just as important to see the human behind the employee. The late Fred Rogers of *Mister Rogers' Neighborhood* was once asked by TV journalist Charlie Rose in an interview: "How many kids do you think are out there who in 30 years you've influenced, who you've made a difference for and who you made them feel something special?" He used the question to address an even deeper issue for him, replying, "I don't care how many. Even if it's just one. We get so wrapped up in numbers in our society and the most important thing is that we're able to be one to one, you and I, with each other in the moment. If we can be present in the moment with the person that we happen to be in that moment with, that's what's important."[5] Fred Rogers was right. We need to be with people in the moment.

We live in a high-tech world, and healthy leadership is a high-touch job. We are all connected with technology, but healthy leaders ensure they are really connecting. People who lead with love make it a priority to get to know the people behind the role—to be present in the moment with them. One study of 25,000 leaders, for instance, found that the most effective leaders had one thing in common—they expressed a sincere interest in their employees.[6] "Sincere" is the operative word. By knowing who your team members are as people, you can better fulfill their needs to keep them fully engaged and help them grow. You can serve them better.

Lead with Empathy and Compassion

Seeing the human behind the employee starts with empathy and compassion. These are two fundamentally different but closely related concepts. Empathy is an awareness of others' emotions and feelings. Compassion is an emotional response to empathy and creates a desire to help—it converts a feeling into action. A healthy leader taps into these two sides of love to serve employees more completely. When you have empathy for other people, your brain predicts what they'll think, feel, and do. The more familiar the other people are to you, the more efficient your brain predicts their inner struggles. When people are less familiar to you, it can be harder to empathize. You can start building empathy by learning one thing new about each team member each week. Consider entering a recurring, weekly appointment on your calendar reminding you to ask questions so you can learn about the people on your team.

Another strategy for increasing workplace empathy is to walk a day in their shoes. Shadow team members occasionally so that you really know what a day is like for them—the challenges, stresses, and joys they encounter. When you know the person and their story, both inside and outside work, it is much easier to demonstrate empathy and compassion. We can then help team members address challenges so they can grow.

In addition to shadowing and regular check-ins with team members, one way to cultivate empathy and compassion within your team is to start each team meeting with a quick "High/Low" around the group. The team leader starts by stating one "High" (something positive that happened) and one "Low" (something negative that happened) since the last meeting.

The Highs and Lows can be personal or work-related. Each person in the group does the same around the table or the call. For instance, a leader's High might be that her daughter just won a piano competition, and a Low might be that a key player decided to leave the company. A team member's High could be that he hit last week's deadline and was under his expense budget, while the Low could be that his father was just diagnosed with cancer.

Our clients have found it to be a valuable window into the worlds of their team members. It creates real-time opportunities to support employees who need help; for instance, lending resources to get a project back on track or having dinner sent home during trying times. The sharing of Highs enables you to recognize people for positive contributions, such as the time they spent over the weekend serving the needy or going the extra mile to recover a customer who had left. The sharing of Lows helps build empathy within your team and enables you to show compassion by taking supportive actions.

You make a living by what you get,
but you make a life by what you give away.

Respect People and Perspectives

Before you show your team members compassion, you must first show them the most basic form of respect: acknowledging them and their perspectives. Simply acknowledging someone and their challenges can make things better even if it cannot make things right.

Many well-intentioned leaders often fall short in this area. It's not that they don't want to respect every person in their organization. Rather, most leaders today are burdened with constant meetings, glued to their phones fielding messages, and generally overwhelmed by the sheer number of people they must engage with each day. Amid such demands, it's understandable to cut corners in your interactions with others, since opting out of certain interactions isn't necessarily overtly disrespectful. But healthy leadership requires us to go the extra mile to always acknowledge our team members whenever possible. It's a way of saying, "I respect you."

Dr. Patrick Quinlan served as CEO of Ochsner Health System in New Orleans for 11 years. During his tenure as the head of this large health-care provider, he instituted a policy that became known as the "10-5 Way." The rule was straightforward. If employees were within 10 feet of another person, they made eye contact and smiled. But if they were within five feet, they said hello.[7] Did this respectful gesture of acknowledgment require great time and effort? Not at all. It only took building a new organization-wide habit, whose impact on the company was not just noticeable but measurable, too. Quinlan saw civility proliferate throughout the offices, while patient satisfaction scores rose in tandem with new referrals. The takeaways: First, you must acknowledge other's presence before you can acknowledge their importance; second, when you show love to others, they show it right back.

To adopt the "10-5 Way" (or a similar approach) into your organization, start by establishing norms of respectful acknowledgment for everyone to follow. You, the leader, must model these norms first and foremost. The key to implementing a rule like this, however, is to avoid presenting it as a cumbersome obligation, or as one more line added to employees' job descriptions. Instead, emphasize the motivation behind the approach: respect. The goal is for every team member to feel acknowledged and that they are being treated with dignity. As the poet Maya Angelou once said, "People will forget what you said, people will forget what you did, but people will never forget how you made them feel."

Tame Your Technology

In our increasingly fast, tech-driven world, it is especially important to establish respectful norms related to both the virtual workplace and our phone use. Screens exert a magnetic force on our attention, leading us to disengage from others in ways we never did before smartphones and constant notifications.

How many times have you seen someone abruptly withdraw from a conversation because of the ding of a phone? You've probably done it yourself, just like we have. In pre-smartphone times, this type of behavior would have negatively stood out. *Did you see how John just checked out of the conversation for two minutes?* someone might have whispered after a meeting. Yet today most of us are accustomed, or even desensitized, to this happening at the workplace, both in in-person settings and in remote interactions. But let's be honest: No one likes being on the receiving end of such inattention and distraction. Why? Because we don't feel acknowledged or respected. Healthy leaders need to be the ones to lead the way when it comes to taming their technology, thus preventing it from disrupting an environment anchored by love.

Acknowledging people is the principle of love in action. When healthy leaders make this a part of their everyday behavior, it has a positive ripple effect on the team and even redefines interactions with customers, as it did at Ochsner Health System. This will produce tangible benefits. As studies on retail behavior have demonstrated, acknowledging potential customers with a friendly greeting increases both sales and customer satisfaction. In short, good business begins with a simple "Hello."

Listen to Understand

Another habit that healthy leaders adopt to demonstrate respect is one that is harder than it seems: listening effectively. Leaders who listen well make it a priority to listen first. They listen to understand rather than to respond. This allows them to truly discover what is important to the other person, which should in turn be important to the leader. A healthy listening practice to cultivate is to *not* talk, even in your own head, when you're most tempted to. Listen to understand, not to respond or to judge. Replace judgment with curiosity about people, projects, perspectives, etc.

Healthy leaders value the person without having to agree with everything the other party says or does. They balance conviction in their beliefs with compassion for and curiosity about others. They also balance accountability for results with grace for individual circumstances. Listening deeply to your team is so fundamental because it demonstrates respect for the person and their perspectives. As motivational speaker and author Zig Ziglar put it, "Speak in such a way that others love to listen to you. Listen in such a way that others love to speak to you."

When you demonstrate love in the above ways, you will build a solid foundation for a healthy team that generates healthy results for your organization. That's the power of love!

If you have some respect for people as they are, you can be more effective in helping them to become better than they are.

—JOHN W. GARDNER,
former secretary of the U.S. Department of Health, Education, and Welfare

---

Cultivate Healthy Leadership

LOVE
Do what is in the best interest of others

✓ Put the needs of my team before my own.

✓ Conduct regular one-on-one check-ins to get to know the people behind my employees.

✓ Connect with the people who are with me versus being technologically connected with those who are not with me.

✓ Listen to understand, not to respond or to judge. Replace judgment with curiosity about people, projects, perspectives, etc.

My commitment to **Love**:

_____

_____

_____

When you work with love, you bind yourself to yourself, and to one another, and to God . . . Work is love made visible.
—KAHLIL GIBRAN,
from *The Prophet*

3

POSITIVITY

Manage negative emotions and increase positive ones

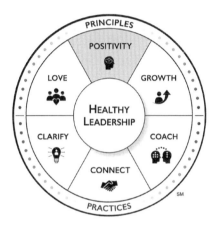

When Sara was a student, she was a terrible test-taker and had a very hard time retaining what she read. At 16 years old, her parents separated, and she lost a close friend who was run over by a car while they were riding bikes together. This trauma, coupled with Sara's learning struggles, created intense emotional and academic obstacles during high school. At one point, Sara's dad handed Sara a set of cassette tapes by Dr. Wayne Dyer called *How to Be a No-Limit Person*. Dyer talked about things like the power of positivity, the ability to visualize and manifest what you want in life, how to embrace failure, and how to train your brain to respond to life's challenges in a way that propels you forward instead of holding you back. In short, mindset.[1]

Upon entering the world as an adult, Sara knew what she wanted to do with her life: become an attorney like her father. So, she did what all aspiring lawyers must do after college: take the LSAT. Unfortunately, she did very poorly on her first attempt. Yet she was undeterred. Her father had raised her to see failure as an opportunity to learn from past mistakes and do better in the future, which is what she planned to do. She signed up for a prep class, studied even harder, took the test, and did even worse the second time.

Sara stepped away from her dream of becoming a lawyer. Even so, she didn't stop dreaming about a great career, though her life certainly wasn't turning out to be the success story she had imagined. After a short-lived job as a chipmunk at Disney World, she got a job selling fax machines. Going door-to-door, trying to convince strangers to listen to her sales pitch, was no walk in the park. Doors were slammed in her face, sometimes she broke down in tears, and a few times the police were even called on her. But still, she didn't give up. She understood that she could benefit from these seemingly negative experiences. She knew she could control how she thought about the challenges she faced. As she later remembered, "During my fax-selling stint, I would spend much of my free time trying to figure out what I really wanted out of life and what my strengths were. I knew I was good at selling and that I eventually wanted to be self-employed. I thought, instead of fax machines, I'd love to sell something that I create and actually care about."[2]

And that's just what she did. After seven years selling fax machines, Sara realized that women needed a better kind of "shapewear" than old-fashioned stockings. So, she founded her own company, Spanx, and used the sales skills she'd honed going door to door to sell her products. This is how Sara Blakely became the self-made billionaire she is today. And she credits this incredible success in large part to what her father taught her about the power of positivity. As Blakely puts it, "I'm now the founder and

CEO of Spanx, a company I built from scratch with $5,000 in savings. It wasn't because I aced all my classes in school—it was because I studied the art of mindset."[3]

Positivity changes us for the better, and it builds psychological strengths. Research shows that people who experience more positivity become more optimistic, open, and driven by a sense of purpose. Positivity further helps to build good mental habits and spurs people to find multiple pathways toward a goal or through a problem. Even an individual's resilience is improved with positivity because people can bounce back from challenges more quickly. Positivity also helps people create and strengthen social connections. It leads you to build more and better relationships. Finally, positivity improves physical health by reducing stress hormones and increasing brain chemicals that result in decreased inflammation and improved immune functioning.[4] Positivity is medicine for our minds, bodies, and lives.

Leader as Light

All living organisms move toward things that are life-sustaining and away from those that are life depleting. We see this in action when the plant on our windowsill moves toward the sunlight. Light activates chemical reactions in plants and people that generate life-giving energy. This movement toward light is called the heliotropic effect.[5]

It's a good bet that most if not all of the best leaders in your life have filled you with positive energy and emotions. Healthy leaders act in ways that draw people to them, such as inspiring others, showing integrity, and being genuine in their interactions and relationships. Healthy leaders supply light so that teams can ultimately shine on their own. Employees who work for healthy leaders tend to be more engaged in their work, have an improved sense of well-being, and are more innovative.[6]

Let's look at how you can increase positivity by managing your mind, talking yourself up, and encouraging others.

Manage Your Mind

Your mind can be your best friend or your worst enemy. It can liberate you or imprison you. We know more than ever that how we think and feel directly affects our brain and body. Effective mind management supports sound mental and physical health. Your intangible mind, which includes thoughts and emotions, changes your tangible brain. To better manage your mind, let's first get a better understanding of how the brain works.

The human brain is the most complex three pounds in the universe. Picture one of those airline flight route maps with a massive web that connects hundreds of points of destination. It is a blur of lines going every which direction. Now, multiply that image by one billion and you are starting to get close to what your vast neural network looks like. The human brain contains approximately 128 billion neurons. Each neuron is connected to 10,000 others. It's quite a map. Brain-imaging research has proven that the brain is neuroplastic, meaning it can change and grow new neural connections. With repetition, your thoughts that fire together get wired together. To change your mind, you need to change your emotions and thoughts. First, let's look at emotions.

When experiencing an emotion, it physiologically lasts for around 90 seconds. However, we often feel it much longer as we ruminate over, or replay, that emotion. For example, if a big project at work goes poorly, you experience the disappointing emotion in that moment. The experience itself is over, but you might continue thinking about it for days, weeks, months, or even years. Your rumination is creating a stronger neural connection associated with that situation. Your negative emotions also limit possibilities you see.[7] When we are enraged, frustrated, or overwhelmed, our peripheral vision narrows, along with our cognitive vision. Just think of a time when you felt really overwhelmed with a project at work. The brain's natural reaction to this negative feeling was to become narrower and more focused. When filled with negative emotion, we tend to see fewer options or solutions.

To help manage your negative emotions, begin with a practice Dr. Dan Siegel, clinical professor of psychiatry at the UCLA School of Medicine, calls "name it to tame it." The act of noticing and identifying the emotion helps to create some distance between the emotion and the intense feelings that accompany it. Doing so allows you to pause and use your breath to help calm your physiology. According to David Rock, co-founder and CEO of the NeuroLeadership Institute, you can reduce stress by up to 50 percent by simply noticing and naming your emotional state.[8] Ensure that you express the emotion as a passing feeling, not a defined state. For example, instead of saying, "I am sad" (a defined state), a better option is to say, "I feel sad" (a fleeting emotion).

Positive emotions help you see opportunities for growth and improvement, as demonstrated by psychology professor and researcher Barbara Fredrickson's "broaden and build theory." Positive emotions facilitate clear thinking about options and enable us to be creative, playful, and curious.[9] Simply recalling a joyful memory or receiving a small gift can make a difference in your ability to develop creative solutions to daily challenges we face. In fact, Cornell University scientists studied how physicians diagnosed a patient with liver disease by having him think aloud so they could hear their reasoning and the alternatives they considered. When physicians were given a small gift—a bag of candy—those physicians were better at integrating case information. They were also less likely to fixate on their initial ideas and develop a premature diagnosis.[10] So, whether you make a nice gesture or give a small gift, creating positive emotions can serve you well during your next doctor's appointment or any other meeting you have.

Mental Framing Tools

You can go three weeks without food, three days without water, and three minutes without oxygen. But you can't go three seconds without a thought.[11] In fact, we average 30,000 to 50,000 thoughts per day. With all of this unceasing mental activity between your ears, what do you do with negative thoughts that inevitably pop into your mind? The key to changing thoughts is to replace them with others, since you can't just force a negative thought out of your mind. Ask yourself, "Is this thought serving me?" If not, shifting perspectives is an effective strategy. Let's explore two tools to help shift your perspective.

First, take a third-party perspective by giving yourself advice as if you were a good friend. Begin by using your own name. For example, say to yourself, "Julie, all your past experiences tell me that you will do a great job with this upcoming board meeting. You have done this 100 times. You've got this!" This creates psychological distance between you and the situation to help you see it more clearly, while keeping it personal by using your own name.

The second tool is "mental time travel." This helps put your thoughts into perspective by reflecting on how you will feel about the situation you currently face in one week, one month, one year. Will it still feel like such a big deal in the future? This allows your brain to simulate the healing power of time and gain the bigger perspective that it provides. As a result, you can feel more positive emotions. This expands your ability to see more options through the wisdom of future perspective, which in turn can help you deal with the current setback. Mental framing tools help us create time and space between the situation and ourselves, so we can shift perspectives and consider more solutions.[12]

Nothing in the world is good or bad, but you make it so.
—WILLIAM SHAKESPEARE
from *Hamlet*

Talk Yourself Up

You talk more to yourself than to anyone else in the world. You are the only one who is with you 100 percent of the time. The conversations you have with yourself have an overwhelmingly high impact on your mindset compared to conversations with others. If you are not your biggest cheerleader, you might just be your biggest enemy.

To better understand the tone of your inner dialogues, begin by asking yourself, "Would I talk to my best friend the way I talk to myself?" or "Am I giving the support, confidence, and hope to myself that I give to others?" Most people realize that they are much harder on themselves than others. If you talked to others the way you talk to yourself, your friendships would change, and you would likely have fewer friends. Instead, Julie gives herself real high fives. She says, "Good job, Jules!" and slaps her palms together high in the air to reinforce self-positivity, congratulating herself for a job well done, from the outcome of a coaching discussion to finishing the laundry. A simple high five can help with self-motivation and positively affect your self-evaluation.[12] Cheer for yourself the way you would for your favorite sports team or your child during a competitive event. You are always with yourself, so encouragement and affirmation are always options for your internal conversations . . . if you choose.

In the face of challenging circumstances (and we all have our share), the words you choose for that conversation with yourself will directly impact how long you will find yourself in those situations. Use your words to change your situation, not to describe it. The moment you speak something—good or bad—you give birth to it as an idea, an expectation, or a desire. By controlling what you say and how you say it—using positive words with enthusiasm—you help to change your physical and mental state.

We remember the year we started our business. We spent a lot of time talking ourselves up. Like most start-up businesses, we had our share of challenges, disappointments, and adjustments. We recall many well-intended friends asking, "Hey, how's your business coming along?" We could have described our situation by saying, "Gee, it's been a tough year. We have had to really dig into our savings to keep things going and it's been a lot harder than we thought it would be to convert existing business relationships into paying customers. Also, it's a lot more work than we thought it would be." That type of response would not only drag our friends down, it would have also planted the seeds of doom for our business. Instead, we chose to use words to change our situation. We talked ourselves up in response to friends' inquiries. We reframed our situation and said things like, "We feel good about our prospects and are confident that we are doing the right things that will pay off long-term. Most importantly, we are passionate about our work, and that's a victory." Our words planted the seeds of the success that was to come. Tell people how you *want* to feel, and it won't be long before you do.

You can also choose your words to reframe your perspective. Small words can change the way we see the world and can even be mind-changing. For example, think of something you *have to* do today. Maybe you have to take out the trash, you have to recruit a new team member, or you have to make an important presentation to a customer. Now, whatever it is you *have to* do, reframe it as something you *get to* do. So now, you get to take out the trash, you get to recruit a new team member, or you get to make an important presentation to a customer. How does changing one word change your perspective? If you are like most people, it turns an obligation (have to) into appreciation (get to). When thinking about "getting to" do something, your mind becomes filled with gratitude (a positive emotion). You can quickly think through all the reasons that you are fortunate to "get to" do something that you either took for granted or disliked doing. A one-word difference can change your perspective and your world.

Encourage Others

Although it's an ambitious goal to change the world as a whole, we often underestimate our singular power to positively change the world for those around us. While we might not all be Gandhi, Mother Teresa, or Martin Luther King, Jr., each of us has the power to change someone's world with the gift of encouragement. Whether it's a conversation with an employee, colleague, boss, friend, or relative, or simply placing an order at a restaurant, every word makes a difference. The results of our interactions are rarely neutral; they are almost always positive or negative. Ask yourself, "Do my words, energy, and body language reflect my desire to encourage others and be a positive influence?"

Your words create your world. Humans are unique in that we can comfort each other with words. A compliment at the end of a hard day can calm you down while a hateful word from someone can cause your brain to think there is a threat, thus stimulating negative emotions. Words do not even have to be spoken to have an impact. Text messages can change a person's heart rate, breathing, and metabolism. Words have a physical effect on your body because various brain regions that process language also control major organs and regulatory systems.[14]

Words can create a lasting impact. They change not just how we feel but what we see as possible for our lives. In fact, a Korn Ferry Institute study found that 65 percent of female CEOs from large companies only realized they could attain that position after someone told them they could.[15] Knowing that words can have such life-changing power, it's interesting to learn that the English language contains 62 percent negative emotional words and only 38 percent positive emotional words. So, choose your words carefully. The English language stacks the deck toward negativity. You must intentionally choose your words to be a positive force for your team.

Share Strength Stories

One exercise that encourages you and others is to share "strength stories." During strength stories, team members share a verbal narrative about a time when they were at their very best. Have them conjure details of that time: what they were doing, who they were interacting with, what they accomplished, and how they felt. As each person shares their story, observe the joy they express and the joy that others feel as they listen to the story. This exercise helps you savor the past and deepen your understanding of your strengths. As an additional benefit, strength stories connect all parties with a shared positive experience in the moment and well into the future.

Positive, encouraging words are the seeds of success. Plant those seeds in someone's mind and heart today. You'll start a positive ripple effect that will be felt by many people and many miles away, not to mention the positive effect you will feel inside. Speak words of strength, opportunity, kindness, and appreciation to bring out the best in yourself and others.

Language is very powerful.
Language does not just describe reality.
Language creates the reality it describes.
—DESMOND TUTU,
theologian and human rights activist

Take the Gratitude Challenge

Words of gratitude can also change your world. Try this twist on a gratitude journal. Each day for the next two weeks, write three good things that happened **and** how *you* contributed. If you do the following gratitude challenge, you will experience positive benefits, including increased happiness and decreased depressive symptoms that can last up to six months.[16] Simply type it into your phone's notepad or go old school and write it on paper like this . . .

Day	3 Good Things that Happened Today . . .	How I Contributed . . .
1	▪ My son came home from college to spend the weekend with me. ▪ My elderly neighbor was thrilled to see the new flowers in her garden. ▪ My best friend is feeling better about her job search.	▪ I paid for his flight. ▪ I helped plant the flowers. ▪ I talked with her, calmed her down, and shared some tools to help her.

Alternatively, write a letter of gratitude to a person in your life each week for three weeks. Research has shown significant changes in positive neural activity with practices such as these.[17] For a quicker boost of gratitude for your team, use a real or virtual gratitude wall where notes of gratitude and thanks are written for all to see.

Healthy leaders manage their minds, talk themselves up, and encourage others. They become a light that shines on those around them.

Feeling gratitude and not expressing it
is like wrapping a present and not giving it.
—WILLIAM ARTHUR WARD,
motivational writer

Cultivate Healthy Leadership

POSITIVITY
Manage negative emotions and increase positive ones

✓ Express my emotions as a passing feeling, not a defined state. (I feel sad vs. I am sad.)

✓ Put my thoughts and emotions into perspective by giving myself advice and relaying it the same way I would to my best friend.

✓ Replace "I have to" with "I get to" to create positive feelings of gratitude.

✓ For two weeks, write three good things that happened and how you contributed to those good things happening.

✓ Create a real or virtual gratitude wall where notes of gratitude and thanks are written for all to see.

My commitment to **Positivity**:

_____

_____

_____

Change your mind, and it changes everything.

4

GROWTH

Seek new insights, knowledge, and skills

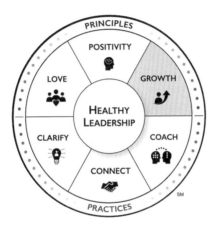

After many years of hard work, Manfred Steiner finally achieved his lifelong goal: He defended his Ph.D. dissertation and received his doctorate in physics from Brown University. But unlike the other students in his graduating class at the Ivy League institution, he didn't plan on using his prestigious degree to launch his professional life. After all, as a medical doctor with a prior Ph.D. in biochemistry, he'd already enjoyed a long and successful career as a hematologist. See, Steiner was 89 years old when he attained his second doctorate in 2021.[1] Why did he do it? Because he had always been fascinated by physics and simply wanted to continue learning.

While on the surface Steiner's story might appear to have nothing to do with business, in fact it has everything to do with healthy leadership. Like Steiner, healthy leaders are lifelong and everyday learners. They are insatiably curious about their organization, teams, and industry. One goal of learning and growing is to increase our capacity to integrate insights from a wide range of ideas. Steiner had many perspectives upon which to draw. An added benefit of this type of learning is that when you grow, you can better help others grow. And when you help others grow, you grow, too. It's a positive upward spiral.

Healthy leaders have what pioneering psychologist Carol Dweck famously called a "growth mindset." As she describes it, "In a growth mindset, people believe that their most basic abilities can be developed through dedication and hard work—brains and talent are just the starting point. This view creates a love of learning and a resilience that is essential for great accomplishment."[2] Practice building a growth mindset with one powerful word: yet. If you do not know or understand something, tell yourself, "I don't have this skill yet." Or "I don't understand this topic yet." Using "yet" plants seeds of growth and learning in your mind instead of accepting the current state as the future state (e.g., I don't have this skill and therefore I never will). Growth-minded leaders believe their talents can be developed through constant learning, hard work, and input from others.

Take the case of Microsoft CEO Satya Nadella, who succeeded Steve Ballmer as the leader of the company. Nadella dramatically revived Microsoft's reputation and its relevance by emphasizing collaboration. He ignited what he calls a "learn-it-all" culture, which is in stark contrast to the company's historical "know-it-all" culture. As Harry McCracken explains in the article Microsoft Rewrites the Code, ". . . the results have been eye-popping: more than $250 billion in market value gains in less than four years."[3]

Your team looks to you as its role model for leading, yes, but also for learning and growing. So, what do they see? Does it look to them like you know it all, like you're stuck, or like you're just cruising? Hopefully not. If your team sees a thirst for growth in you, they will demonstrate the same behavior. They will see a leader whose continual growth hones their competence . . . and competence builds confidence. Confidence is critical; healthy leaders need it, and their teams want to see it.

Simple Truths of Growth

Here are five truths about growth that we have identified during our many years of work:

Change is inevitable, but growth is a choice. Change is omnipresent, but if we resist it, we may not grow from it. Real and sustained growth happens when we choose it.

What gets watered grows. When we reinforce ourselves or others for a certain behavior, that behavior will be performed more frequently. Since reinforcement feels good, we do more of what feels good.

Growth almost always occurs when we are uncomfortable. Even if we initiate growth phases ourselves, growth by its nature pushes our thoughts, words, and/or actions into new, uncharted territory, which means we must confront uncertainty. Those who are growth-oriented learn to embrace discomfort.

When we help others grow, we grow. Just as when we teach, we learn, when we cultivate growth in others, we also plant seeds of growth within ourselves. It creates a virtuous cycle. We also tend to feel great satisfaction and fulfillment from helping others grow.

Growth opportunities are limitless. Growth is not a finite entity like a plot of land with limited square footage. There is always more room to grow. Our mindset will either reveal or hide growth opportunities for us.

With these five truths about growth in mind, next we will share strategies to help you and your team grow.

We cannot become what we need to be by remaining what we are.

—MAX DE PREE,
founder, Herman Miller office furniture

Become an Expert on You

We can only improve what we observe and are aware of. So, knowledge of yourself is the most important type of knowledge—and provides the most fertile ground for self-growth. Knowing your own tendencies, preferences, natural gifts, and weaknesses helps you be more personally effective and, as a result, a more insightful and effective leader. You must know yourself to lead others in a healthy way. Self-aware leaders intentionally work to minimize their blind spots—which are the behaviors, traits, or tendencies that others see but you are unaware of. Picture the friend who thinks he is a great listener, but everyone else wishes he would stop talking constantly.

Blind spots are so central to leadership performance that they have attracted scientific researchers. David Zes and Dana Landis analyzed 6,977 assessments of managers and executives to identify blind spots. They compared the assessment results to the financial data of the 486 publicly traded companies for which the subjects worked. After tracking stock performance over 30 months, the researchers found that organizations with a higher percentage of self-aware leaders (fewest blind spots) had the strongest financial performance. Meanwhile, companies with the least self-aware leaders (most blind spots) had the lowest financial performance.[4] In other words, self-knowledge isn't just good leadership. It's good business.

Prevent blind spots and build self-awareness by asking your team what you can Start, Stop, and Keep doing to help them succeed . . . and carefully listen to their answers—with humility, not defensiveness. This process is simple on the mind, but it can be tough on the heart, not to mention on your pride. It takes courage to ask for feedback and potentially uncover blind spots, but the cost of low self-awareness is your leadership credibility. Healthy leaders also prevent blind spots by making concerted efforts to seek unfiltered truths about their organization, their challenges, their opportunities, and most importantly, about their leadership. The higher you are in an organization, the more filtered the information you receive. It's a natural and predictable phenomenon, but it's also a precarious position to be in. No leader wants to be "the emperor who wore no clothes," so staying connected with frontline team members enables you to access unfiltered information about your leadership.

Healthy leaders listen and learn more than they talk and tell, they question assumptions more than they assert them, and they push beyond their comfort zone more than they seek comfort. Also, armed with self-awareness, you can more clearly see your weaknesses so you can build a team with strengths that complement your weaknesses.

Create Mental Space

As you capture data about the impact of your leadership, before acting on it you must create mental space to reflect on it, filter through it, and identify patterns and root causes of others' perceptions. The hyper-speed nature of today's information-saturated, time-deprived world forces us to run, run, run—and this is just to keep pace. Today's mobile technology can be a double-edged sword. It is a blessing in terms of your productivity, but it is a curse on your ability to be still and know yourself. You can end up being a "human doing" rather than a human being, which leaves no time for reflection and awareness.

We can think about our own thinking by the time we are nine years old, so in today's hyperactive and attention-demanding world, how can you spend more time thinking about your thinking? Our youngest daughter has a special area in her room where she can chill and relax. She calls it her "chillax zone." Although your "chillax zone" might not have big pink pillows and a fluffy white carpet like our daughter's, you too need to reserve a time and place that provides mental space. Your space can be your car as you drive home after work, a reading or meditation corner in your house, your bathtub, your gym, a nearby park where you walk; your space can be anywhere you can be alone with your thoughts. The thinking, planning, and reflection you do in this space helps you get out of the daily trenches and elevate up to the eagle's nest. This provides a broader and clearer perspective on yourself, your work, your purpose, your values, your team, and your life.

Here are two other proven ways to create mental space that can help you grow and be your best. First, keep a journal. James Pennebaker, a liberal arts professor of psychology at the University at Texas in Austin, has spent 40 years researching the link between writing and processing emotions. In studies, he has divided people into two groups, asking some to jot down emotionally charged experiences, and others to write about whatever daily occurrence popped into their mind. Both groups were tasked with writing for about 20 minutes, three days in a row. Pennebaker found that the people who wrote about their emotionally charged episodes experienced the most improvement in their physical well-being. They had lower blood pressure, better immunity, and visited the doctor less frequently. They were also less depressed, generally happier, and less anxious.[5]

Unexpressed emotions do not go away. They eventually rear their heads in uglier ways. Journaling is a good way to gain a new perspective on your thoughts and emotions. Writing is more visceral and tied to your emotions than typing, so this is one time you want to go old school and write down your thoughts. Write anything that comes to mind about an emotionally charged event. Next, write what you learned from this event and how it has helped you grow or how it can help you grow in the future.

Second, dedicate time for strategic tasks. Strategic tasks require higher-order thinking, focused attention, reasoning, and creativity. Set aside 45 minutes of uninterrupted time to work on this during your peak hours of attention. To stay focused, keep a physical or digital notepad by your side. When working on your strategic tasks, jot down unrelated thoughts that come to mind. Also, silence distractions, including email and text notifications.

Strategic tasks require conscious effort and draw upon your brain's executive function, which has limited capacity. As a result, multitasking on strategic tasks decreases productivity up to 40 percent, decreases quality of work, and increases negative emotions associated with the task. It can take your brain more than 20 minutes to fully focus on the current task and for "residue" from the previous task(s) to fade away. In fact, cognitive neuroscientist Sandra Chapman, founder of the Center for BrainHealth, says, "We're learning that multitasking is to the brain as cigarette smoking is to the lungs. Chronic multitaskers have shallower thinking and may be less able to see the bigger picture."[6] As you work on your strategic tasks or any other tasks, create mental space during your workday by taking 5-minute brain breaks five times. Walk away from your workspace, take deep breaths, and let your mind wander.

You must learn to be still in the midst of activity
and to be vibrantly alive at rest.

—INDIRA GANDHI,
former Prime Minister of India

Cultivate Curiosity

Best practices for leading are everywhere, and often the best ones don't come from the world of business. For example, observe the leaders in your life outside of work. You might find nuggets of leadership excellence from a parent, an in-law, a clergy member, a speaker at a professional association meeting, a friend, a stranger you follow on social media, your child's school principal, a Scout troop leader, or a particularly helpful manager at a local store. Healthy leadership is everywhere. Watch, ask, listen, and learn.

There are also lessons to be learned in everything your team does. Look for learning opportunities in post-project reviews, customer meetings, conflicts with other departments, changes in priorities, miscommunications, and mistakes. Get curious about these situations. This will also set a positive example for your employees and plant the seeds of curiosity in them. Try these five strategies to cultivate curiosity for you and your team.

Seek novelty. Humans naturally seek and enjoy novelty. Novelty is good for us and helps us create new neural connections. Try something for the first time, explore new experiences. For some, this may be skydiving or bungee jumping, but you can also reach new heights on the ground. Consider things that stretch you, such as: taking an improv or painting class; hiking a new trail in your area; learning a new sport (we started playing pickleball recently); or trying a new recipe with unfamiliar ingredients. Even new puzzles, card games, or board games can infuse novelty into your day.

Find a mentor. Mentors are a great source of growth and an ideal place to quench your curiosity about the future. If experience truly is the best teacher, then you would be wise to study the life lessons and expertise of a mentor. For the greatest benefit, seek out mentors with the specific skills you desire to acquire. Maybe it's your organization's top strategist, the salesperson with the magnetic people skills, or the teammate who is consistently a top performer. Mentors can be older or younger than you. Younger mentors may not have as much experience in the field, but they can also offer fresh insights, tools, and perspectives.

Ask questions. Questions are a shortcut to learning and growing. Tap back into your childhood curiosity, which is very useful in adulthood. Start with two simple questions.

1. *Can you tell me more?* Most people are not as thorough in their replies as the curious mind requires, so ask others to share more about the topic or situation to help you see a more complete picture.

2. *Why?* Consider the number of times you've heard children ask "Why, why, why?" This question gets to the heart of a childlike curiosity and deeper understanding. Why did we get that result? Why does this process have these steps? Why are we doing project X this way? Why does this matter for the organization? Why does it take X days to complete this task? Why are we measuring this? Finding the answer to such questions is fantastic, but the mental growth that comes from regularly straining to untangle hard *why* questions is even more important.

Identify patterns. Look for patterns or themes among people, problems, and situations. This will help you gain a deeper understanding of underlying dynamics that are the root cause for the way people perform, the reason problems exist, and the way situations play out. You'll uncover transferable insights that are applicable in other contexts in the future.

Picking out patterns in this fashion also helps create new neural pathways to keep your brain growing and active.

Create learning goals. It's smart to have performance goals identifying what you want to achieve. In addition, healthy leaders establish learning goals that identify specific skills or knowledge they want to develop. Achieving a learning goal typically increases your personal capacity to achieve performance goals in the future. For example, a leader might have a performance goal of implementing a new system within budget and on time. She might also have a learning goal to improve her communication and project management skills. Clearly, achieving her learning goals will better enable her and her team to achieve the performance goal of implementing the new system. In fact, in a study published in the *Academy Management Executive*, researchers used a business simulator to test the effects of learning goals for sales professionals. According to their results, "Performance was highest for individuals with a specific, high-learning goal. The market share achieved by those with a learning goal was almost twice as high as those with a performance outcome goal."[7] This is not an "either-or" proposition; rather, it's an "and-both" proposition. Set specific performance goals (more on this in Chapter 7: Coach) and set specific learning goals.

Learning is the oxygen of human growth.

Learn from Adversity

Most growth occurs when you are uncomfortable. That's why adversity can be our friend in growth. Since adversity has an uncanny knack for paralyzing us, it becomes critical to keep moving through it. Otherwise, we will be stalled in its grip.

At 19, Amy Purdy was living the life she had always dreamed of as a massage therapist, snowboarder, and avid traveler. Then, the unthinkable occurred. She caught a strain of bacterial meningitis. In no time she was comatose in a hospital on life support, with a 2 percent chance of survival. Miraculously, she beat the illness, but not without life-altering losses: her spleen, her two kidneys, and both her legs. When she was discharged from the hospital, the unwieldy prosthetic legs she was given didn't fill her with hope—only despair. As she later recalled, "I was absolutely physically and emotionally broken. But I knew that in order to move forward, I had to let go of the old Amy and embrace the new Amy."

Despite the lightning bolt of adversity that had struck her, Amy started piecing her life back together, and she did so fearlessly and creatively. She soon went back to work and school, created special legs for herself (with neon-pink duct tape) so that she could return to snowboarding, and she founded a nonprofit to help other young people with disabilities pursue action sports. Not only that, she went on to compete as a snowboarder at the Paralympics, where she brought home multiple medals. She later published a book while also competing in an even more public way, on the TV show *Dancing with the Stars*. Looking back now, Amy says that she would never change what happened to her because she sees it as a "magnificent gift." The loss of her legs "enabled" her, in her words, to discover new depths of imagination and resourcefulness in herself.[8]

Amy Purdy's response to her devastating circumstance is inspiring, and it is not as uncommon as you might think. Psychologists have found that even when experiencing trauma, most people return to normal levels of functioning, and many actually grow and improve from the trauma. Only a small percentage experience post-traumatic stress disorder. Humans evolved to be naturally resilient in the face of adversity. This explains why Amy and so many others like her can display what is known as post-traumatic growth.[9]

You decide what adversity means to you and how you will use it. Healthy leaders choose to let adversity refine them instead of letting it define them. Healthy leaders learn from the valleys of life so they can reach higher peaks. Here are three specific actions to help you learn and grow through adversity.

Take Inventory

Even in the worst situations—a victim of a natural disaster, prisoner of war, target of abuse, or when hit by a string of unfortunate circumstances—it is easier and natural to focus on what is lost. It could be a home, a relationship, security, freedom, or good health. When we experience adversity, and we all experience it as some point, we tend to think all is lost. Instead, take inventory of what is changed and what is still the same. Acknowledging what remains and is the same helps broaden your perspective. Then, express your gratitude for what remains. An attitude of gratitude creates happier, more resilient people and leaders. Helen Keller's observation sums it up, "When one door of happiness closes, another opens; but often we look so long at the closed door that we do not see the one which has opened for us."

Consider many of the hard-hit, locally owned restaurants during the COVID-19 pandemic. Sure, they were shocked at first when their customers were at home sheltering in place. Then, many of them were able to take inventory of what they still had: loyal customers, a kitchen, and food. With what remained, they pivoted to takeout, delivery, and outdoor dining. Years later, these alternative offerings borne out of crisis have now become an important part of their ongoing business. When adversity hits, similar to what happened to your local restaurant owners, take inventory and comfort in what remains.

Convert Turning Points into Learning Points

Use your experiences of adversity as learning moments to pinpoint opportunities to improve, reflect, grow, rebuild, or test your own character or faith. Instead of, "Why is this happening to me?" ask yourself, "What is the situation trying to teach me?" The pathway to healthy leadership is not always smooth. Sometimes struggles are exactly what you need in life to grow. If you go through life without any obstacles, you won't be as strong as you could be. Think about how your struggles have made you a stronger person and a better leader. There will be challenges along the way. The key is to use them to help you and your team change, learn, and grow.

A young boy born in 1809 is a wonderful example of converting turning points into learning points to benefit millions of people. It was 1818 in France, and Louis, a nine-year-old boy, was sitting in his father's workshop. The father was a harness maker and the boy loved to watch him work the leather.

"Someday, father," said Louis, "I want to be a harness maker, just like you."

"Why not start now?" said the father. He took a piece of leather and drew a design on it. "Now, my son," he said, "take the hole puncher and a hammer and follow this design, but be careful that you don't hit your hand."

Excited, the boy began to work, but when he hit the hole puncher, it flew out of his hand and pierced one eye, blinding him immediately. Later, sight in the other eye failed. Louis was now totally blind.

A few years later, Louis was sitting in the family garden when a friend handed him a pine cone. As he ran his sensitive fingers over the cone, an idea came to him. He grew excited and began to create an alphabet of raised dots on paper so that the blind could feel and interpret what was written.

Louis Braille opened a whole new world for the blind by converting a turning point into a learning point.

Live in the Present

One of our favorite poems says it best:

> *Yesterday is history,*
>
> *Tomorrow is a mystery,*
>
> *Today is a gift,*
>
> *That's why we call it the Present.*
>
> —Alice Morse Earle

There's an adage in rock climbing called the "three-foot world" in which climbers focus not on the massive rock wall they're attempting to climb, but the problems that are immediately in front of them. Once those are completed, they can move their attention to the next three-foot section of the wall. This mindset has helped climbers reach the top of sheer cliffs, and it can help you live in the present. When faced with adversity, it is easy to get overwhelmed with everything you must do to get back to normal. This can quickly turn into worry, but worry is when your mind forecasts the future (typically inaccurately) and makes it feel like the present. However, staying within your three-foot world—one day, one moment at a time—reduces stress and worry by enabling small, daily progress. This focus on the present allows a new normal to unfold versus trying to force your will to recreate what used to be normal. Yielding to what you cannot control is often liberating. Focusing on what you can control is always empowering.

Sooner or later, we all face some form of adversity. When it hits you or your team, keep moving so you can create your own story of resilience and growth!

Cultivate Healthy Leadership

GROWTH
Seek new insights, knowledge, and skills

✓ Ask my team what I can Start, Stop, and Keep doing to help them succeed, then listen with humility.

✓ Create mental space for me to reflect, think, and plan.

✓ Cultivate my curiosity by seeking novelty, finding a mentor, asking questions, and/or creating learning goals.

✓ Learn from my adversity by taking inventory, converting turning points into learning points, and living in the present.

My commitment to **Growth**:

_____

_____

_____

The more we grow, the more we can grow.

HEALTHY LEADERSHIP
PRACTICES

5

CLARIFY

Crystalize a desired future and motivation to get there

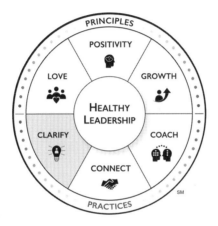

Consider a time at work when you were crystal clear about where your team was going, how you would interact, and what results were expected. If you are fortunate enough to recall such a scenario, you likely worked with more confidence, greater speed, sharper focus, and heightened accountability. This clarity also eliminated or minimized things like waste, anxiety, and fear.

Now, consider a time when your leader's office door was closed more than usual, and she missed the last team meeting. You were trying to get on her calendar, but her assistant pushed your meeting off. During lunch the next day, you start to put two and two together: closed office door plus missed meeting plus inaccessible must mean something BIG is happening.

Oh, no! Is the company being sold? Are they getting ready for a layoff? Am I on the hot seat? Should I start floating my resume?

Your fears turn out to be unfounded. The next week you find out that you were adding two plus two and getting five. Your boss was working on a high-priority, confidential project with a very tight deadline. It required uninterrupted time to focus, so she kept her door closed, opted out of the last meeting, and asked her assistant to defer other meetings. Don't blame yourself for having imagined a disaster scenario; you likely weren't the only employee to do so. To protect and prepare ourselves, we often assume the worst in the absence of evidence to the contrary. Lack of information and unanswered questions can start a Silence Spiral that looks like this:

- Silence leads to doubt;

  - Doubt leads to fear;

    - Fear leads to panic;

      - Panic leads to worst-case thinking.

Particularly when change is on the horizon—as it often is in business and in life—humans crave clarity.

Your brain does not resist change, but it does resist confusion and ambiguity, which often precede change. Your brain seeks information to make sense of the world and to make smart, safe decisions. As a result, when employees don't get the necessary information to perform their jobs or understand the goals of the organization, they tend to fill in the blanks with their own assumptions, and these assumptions are often worst-case scenarios. This is a natural human tendency when we analyze available data in an attempt to seek clarity.

When the Silence Spiral takes hold in an organization, ambiguity rules. This undermines clarity and all of its positive by-products. It can take five minutes or five weeks to play out, but in most cases, the fog of silence rolls in more rapidly than we would imagine. A closed office door, a vague reply to an honest question, or an unreciprocated greeting as you pass in the hallway can trigger the Silence Spiral. The antidote to harmful silence is simple: clarity. It produces calm, trust, and best-case thinking. Clarity is the next best thing to certainty, which is unattainable in our changing world.

Think in Threes

Simplicity facilitates clarity. "Thinking in Threes" is a powerful way to simplify organizational thinking and combat complexity so your team can be crystal clear. As a by-product, it also forces prioritization and focus, and the resulting clarity trickles down the organization. For example, we routinely ask clients to reduce their strategies from perhaps six to three, or to consolidate their values from twelve to three, or to select the three most important business metrics from their laundry list of twenty. No doubt, it's a struggle, but the resulting clarity pays big dividends on many fronts and for years to come.

Truth be told, ending up with precisely three items is less important than the clarity this process creates. For instance, when we encouraged a client to identify just three core values instead of its list of twelve (that no one could remember, let alone implement), they settled on four values. It wasn't necessary to eliminate one more to get down to three values. The benefit was realized—clear articulation of their core values that virtually everyone in the organization now remembers and lives by. Thinking in Threes forces you to create simple, memorable, focused frameworks for your vision, your values, and your performance expectations.

Now, let's discuss actionable steps you can take to clarify your vision, values, and expectations.

Clarify Vision to Inspire Action

About 350 years ago, a shipload of travelers landed on the northeast coast of America. The first year, they established a town site. The next year, they elected a town government. The third year, the town government planned to build a road five miles westward into the wilderness. In the fourth year, the people tried to impeach their town government because they thought it was a waste of public funds to build that road. Who needed to go there anyway?

These were people who had the vision to see 3,000 miles across an ocean and overcome great hardships to get there. But in just a few years, they were not able to see even five miles down the road. They had lost their pioneering spirit, or had they? Had the town council articulated the benefits of the new road—access to the river and a better water supply—the people may well have approved the funds to build the road. Without clear vision, we rarely move beyond our current state. Yet with a clear vision of what we can become, no ocean of difficulty is too great.

That said, be cautious of charging forward too quickly because you might look back and not see your team behind you. As a visionary client once put it, "If you get too far out in front of your troops, you start looking like the enemy." In the distance between you and your team, clarity about the future can turn hazy. Next, we will address how you can bring your people along for the journey.

Fundamental Four Questions

A simple, proven way to clarify your vision and inspire action is to answer the following Fundamental Four questions being asked by your team, *whether you hear them or not*:

1. What are we trying to achieve? (Goals)

2. How are we going to achieve it? (Plans)

3. How can I contribute? (Roles)

4. What's in it for me? (Rewards—professional, social, emotional, and financial)

The clarity of your answers is directly proportionate to the clarity of your vision. If you haven't clearly communicated the answers to all four of these questions, or you assume your team knows the answers, your vision will be a blur. You will have a team going in different directions, unfocused, unclear, or worse, not even wanting to venture a few steps forward.

A clear vision helps teams see where they are going and understand how they can help get there. People naturally feel more accountable and motivated when they clearly understand that they are a part of something bigger than themselves. Commit the time to clarify your vision by answering the Fundamental Four questions . . . and not just once. Maintain clarity by frequently and consistently answering these questions for yourself *and* for your team. It will inspire them to venture to new and exciting destinations with you.

An inspiring leader and our late friend Ron Rossetti liked to say, "Awesomeness is never accidental." Our clients who clarify their vision for their teams are intentional about answering the Fundamental Four questions. They use the questions as a checklist to ensure that their messages address each question. The alignment and engagement in their organizations are notably greater than organizations where employees lack clarity, and their results are notably better.

Rule of Six

One of our clients, Cindy Lewis, is former CEO of AirBorn, a manufacturer of high-quality, custom electronics. She uses the "Rule of Six" when clarifying important information, such as the company's vision. The idea is that you should not expect team members to fully understand or internalize any message until they hear it repeated at least six times. In Lewis' words, "After about six repetitions, we find the concept/message moves to long-term memory and then impacts behavior and habits."[1] This is not a statement about intelligence, but rather a statement about today's information-rich, time-poor, change-intensive world of work. Communicating a message at least six times also forces you to change it up to keep it interesting for your audience (who all have different learning styles) while maintaining the integrity of your message.

With today's data-overloaded, distributed workplace, it can be challenging to decide what to communicate to employees and what to withhold. It's easy to say (usually to yourself), "My team doesn't really need to know all that," or "They won't really understand," or "I don't think they can handle that news right now." Be cautious, because those who underestimate the intelligence or wherewithal of others tend to overestimate their own. You must balance discernment with transparency. Discern what to communicate and what to withhold while being transparent with your team to build trust and engagement . . . and clarity.

If your actions inspire others to dream more, learn more, do more and become more, you are a leader.

—JOHN QUINCY ADAMS,
sixth U. S. President

Clarify Values to Build a Strong Foundation

The Leaning Tower of Pisa is a world-famous tourist attraction, but unlike most architectural landmarks, it isn't because of its breathtaking design. In fact, quite the opposite. Its architect never intended on it being a leaning bell tower. But something went very wrong during its 177 years of construction.

Work on the ground floor of the tower began in 1173. But five years later, the tower began to sink after construction had progressed to the second floor. This was due to a mere three-meter foundation, set in weak, unstable subsoil, and a design that was flawed from the beginning. Similarly, your team's house can only be as strong as the foundation of values you build. Otherwise, you run the risk of the structure tipping to one side, like the Leaning Tower of Pisa.

Values in Action

Values like teamwork, service, integrity, and excellence are just concepts. You cannot measure and manage a concept. However, once you convert your values into actions and behaviors, then you can observe, measure, and manage them. That's how you bring your values to life, by describing, communicating, and modeling behaviors that demonstrate each value. This clarity helps everyone understand the intentions, minimize misinterpretations, and define observable behaviors for which the team is held accountable. Then, your stated values are aligned with your operating values, and you are leading with integrity.

Defining specific, behavioral examples helps clarify the intention of each value. We find that our clients' employees create more specific and more meaningful behavioral examples of values than their leaders would have on their own. In other words, the clarity of healthy leadership doesn't necessarily come from a top-down process where only the leader paints the picture. The team should help paint it, too. Here is a sample values-to-behaviors worksheet that we use with our clients in collaboration with their employees.

Value	Definition	Sample Behaviors	Employee Examples
Integrity	We are personally and professionally responsible to each other, to our customers, and to our shareholders to foster an environment of trust and set the standard for accountability in our industry.	· Disclose misconduct to the appropriate personnel. · Accept responsibility for mistakes. · Keep promises and follow through on obligations. · Take ownership of tasks through completion. · Honor company policies and ethics at all times. · Resolve any conflicts directly with the other person.	Tom in sales raised a potential conflict-of-interest issue with a significant prospect, knowing it might take the company out of consideration for the new business.
Teamwork	By working together with internal and external partners, we generate the greatest impact for all stakeholders—our customers, communities, investors, and ourselves.	· Take advantage of available opportunities to understand how other departments function. · Support the needs of internal and external partners in a timely manner. · Maintain open communication with internal and external partners.	Sara in finance initiated a ride-along with a colleague in sales to better understand his process so she could help resolve a problem reconciling sales bids with actual invoices.

If you really want team values to take root, involve your team in the process of clarifying them. People are committed to what they help create, so let them interpret the values and define behaviors (within your acceptable boundaries). You can facilitate this process by asking questions like:

- What do our team values mean to you?

- What specific behaviors do you think best demonstrate these values?

- What could you do differently to better reflect these values in your work?

Your actions and words are good indicators of your values. If you want these values to be more than just words, team members must perceive them as authentic and live them daily.

The values of leadership shape the behaviors of followers.
—EDWIN G. BOOZ,
co-founder, Booz Allen Hamilton

Make Values-based Decisions

Benjamin Franklin addressed values-based decisions more than two centuries ago when he said, "We stand at a crossroads, each minute, each hour, each day, making choices. We choose the thoughts we allow ourselves to think, the passions we allow ourselves to feel, and the actions we allow ourselves to perform. Each choice is made in the context of whatever value systems we have selected to govern our lives. In selecting that value system, we are in a very real way making the most important choice we will ever make . . . ."[2] Franklin's words still ring true.

Most of us have seen hundreds of sets of organizational and team values plastered on every imaginable surface. Yet all too often, those values are not embedded into daily work and decisions. It's easy to spot values-driven organizations by observing their decision-making processes. Rarely a day goes by without a decision being made that doesn't explicitly relate to one of their values. Using your values to help make decisions clarifies the values for your team.

For example, a Fortune 1000 company made the decision to offer a richer benefits package that would provide employees more choices to meet varying personal needs. These new benefits came with a multimillion-dollar price tag. The Board approved the plan based on the company's core value of "respect for the individual." They realized that the cost of not living their values was ultimately much greater than the cost of the new benefits.

If you don't use your values as tools to guide your decisions and actions, then why have them? If you do not live and practice your team's values, no one else will. So, as you are faced with decisions, use your values as a guidepost to determine your actions. Making values-based decisions sends a strong message about *your* leadership. Take the time to communicate your values; allow your team to personalize them; and most importantly, live them. As a result, your team will work with clarity and alignment.

It's not hard to make decisions
when you know what your values are.

—ROY DISNEY,
director emeritus, The Walt Disney Company

Clarify Expectations to Execute with Excellence

Many of today's leadership practices are rooted in historical military testing, application, and refinement. But what can business leaders gain from current-day military leadership practices—specifically from the U.S. Navy—that have been honed for years? It turns out a lot!

Thanks to his lifelong friend, retired Bob Ernst, U.S. Navy Commander, Lee had the privilege of spending a weekend aboard the USS Abraham Lincoln, about 100 miles off the shore of San Diego, as it prepared for a deployment. This aircraft carrier is the proud flagship of the Navy's fleet. It is like a floating city. Over 5,000 sailors live and work onboard, and the crews perform the most complex flight operations in the most tumultuous conditions—day and night, with absolutely no room for error. Why? Because in this environment, the cost of an error could potentially be tens of millions of dollars in damaged Navy assets or even loss of life. No *Top Gun* movie scenes here. This is the real-life danger zone!

This type of environment demands nothing less than fully synchronized teamwork, passionate selflessness, relentless effort, and consistent execution. All this is delivered by sailors with an average age of 20 years old. Think about it—this peak level of performance is achieved through the work of thousands of young sailors, most of whom did not have a clear direction after graduating high school, never mind an MBA. It is amusing when we contrast this with clients who are frustrated by their highly educated team's performance—a team that is working in a nicely appointed, air-conditioned, land-based office. At the core of this stellar naval performance are crystal-clear expectations.

Expectation Gaps = Execution Gaps

Just as winning in sports starts with practice, winning in business starts with understanding the performance process and expectations. If you wait until after the work is done, you are simply imposing consequences rather than inspiring performance. That's why aligning with your teams on expectations is a good predictor of winning results. The large majority of performance frustrations stem from leaders not clarifying expectations for assigned tasks or projects. Although your team members each have performance expectations for a given role, we are focusing here on the day-to-day, real-time clarity needed to ensure leaders and their teams are in synch. Healthy leaders work side by side with team members to let them know exactly what they expect. This gives team members a clear picture of what success looks like on a given task or project so they can execute with excellence.

The key is to front-load clarity. You and your team should be able to give the same answer to this question: "How will I know if I have met expectations?" Do not rely on others' perceptions of your expectations. Be more specific than you think you need to be. Gaining alignment through clear expectations is job No. 1 for healthy leaders. A good example of clarity in action comes from one of our clients, Encore Wire's Chairman and CEO, Daniel Jones. Jones is crystal clear that 100 percent of orders are shipped within 24 hours of receipt.[3] This expectation is challenging to meet, but it is clear and understood by all employees. Encore team members work together to meet this expectation, which results in a distinctive service advantage within their industry.

As team members embark on new tasks or projects, clarify the 3Ws: What, Who, and When. We use this simple format with our clients to help them drive growth and improvement. The power is in its simplicity.

What	Who	When	Status/Comments
1.			
2.			
3.			

To ensure clear expectations when using the 3Ws, identify only one "Who" per action. Actions with multiple owners tend to become unowned and undone. This simple 3W form is even more effective when you carry it with you as a mental template to bring clarity and closure to daily conversations and interactions. After all, we each bring our own perceptions, experiences, and assumptions to every interaction, so the chance that we will be in sync with others after a discussion is quite low. Since human communication is much more art than science, clarifying the 3Ws after even short conversations helps identify perception gaps and avoid execution gaps.

Timelines vs. Deadlines

The most common type of expectations leaders set are deadlines. This is only natural. We live in a world that trains us to meet deadlines, starting in grade school: your paper is due May 1; finish your community service hours by Aug. 1; faxes are due April 15; the budget is due Nov. 15; your annual goals are due Jan. 15; your payment is due by Feb. 1. Deadlines, deadlines, deadlines. Your team's inherent desire is to meet a deadline to please you, their leader; however, people typically fail to consider timelines *before* committing to deadlines. Healthy leaders focus on timelines (when work gets done) to meet deadlines (when work is due).

Here's an example of what this looks like. It's a Tuesday morning and you say to an employee: "Hey, Ryan, I need this market analysis finalized by Friday noon. It should only take a few hours to clean it up from the last draft you showed me. Can you please do that for me?" Ryan replies, "Sure, I'll take care of it!" Then Ryan goes back to his office, checks his calendar, and says to himself, "Oh, shoot! I didn't realize I had all these commitments and have no available time between now and Friday noon." At this point, the typical response is to go into face-saving and avoidance modes. Ryan believes he cannot go back on his word after he so confidently told you he would take care of it. He also hopes that if he just avoids it, you might forget to ask him for the analysis at noon on Friday. Yes, these responses sound irrational and even ridiculous, but they're very predictable human tendencies in the workplace.

Fast forward . . . when Friday noon arrives, you naturally expect the analysis from Ryan. By 1 p.m., you swing by his office to ask him where it is. Ryan's stomach sinks as he comes clean. You're frustrated because you, like any leader, hate surprises when it comes to missed deadlines and expected deliverables. Ryan does not feel good about his performance, and neither do you. It's a lose-lose situation, as the results are not delivered on time and the relationship credibility is damaged. This is a predictable scenario when you don't ask about your team members' timelines before they commit to deadlines.

Healthy leaders define a vision, establish foundational values, and align expectations. The common denominator to harness all these drivers of success is one thing: clarity.

Cultivate Healthy Leadership

CLARIFY

Crystalize a desired future and motivation to get there

✓ Clarify vision by consistently answering the Fundamental Four questions:
- What are we trying to achieve? (Goals)
- How are we going to achieve it? (Plans)
- How can you contribute? (Roles)
- What's in it for you? (Rewards—professional, social, emotional, and financial)

✓ Clarify values by asking team members:
- What do our team values mean to you?
- What specific behaviors do you think best demonstrate these values?
- What could you do differently to better reflect these values in your work?

✓ Clarify expectations by:
- Using the 3Ws (What, Who, and When) to confirm accountabilities after meetings and interactions.
- Working with team members to consider timelines before committing to deadlines.

My commitment to **Clarify**:

_____

_____

_____

Clarity inspires action.

6

CONNECT

Build ties between work and human needs

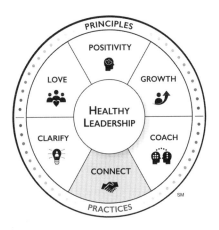

A fter hijacked planes crashed into the Twin Towers in New York City, the Pentagon in Washington, D.C., and a field in Pennsylvania on Sept. 11, 2001, thousands of flights around the world were forced to land at airports that weren't their intended destinations. A whopping thirty-eight of these rerouted planes touched down in the small town of Gander, on the Canadian island of Newfoundland. In a matter of hours, the 10,000-person population of Gander increased by more than half with the arrival of over 6,500 "come from aways," as locals refer to outsiders. But the townspeople chose not to treat the passengers as outsiders. Instead, in a tremendous showing of hospitality, they treated them like new neighbors in need of care and leapt into action.

They opened their homes and schools for the disoriented passengers and provided them with food and places to sleep. Local pharmacists made calls all over the world to make sure the new arrivals got their medications. But they didn't stop there. They also wanted to get to know their guests and have a good time with them. Townspeople organized excursions into nature—after all, why go to Canada if you can't see a moose? They held musical events and huge barbecue cookouts. And most generous of all, they didn't expect anything in return.

After five days, the unplanned social experiment that took form in Gander came to an end when the last of the diverted planes took off. Yet the passengers wanted to return the town's kindness. And indeed, they did, leaving $60,000 in Gander's local suggestion box.

Lifelong bonds were created in Gander the week after Sept. 11. A decade later, hundreds of stranded "plane people" returned to Gander to commemorate the anniversary, remember the tragedy, and visit the friends they had made. In one case, a British man and a Texan woman met, fell in love, and got married after their return. Among those present at the 10th anniversary were Irene Sakoff and David Hein, a couple with a growing list of plays to their name. They spent the anniversary interviewing many of the Gander residents and plane people. Those interviews became the basis of the hit Broadway musical, *Come From Away*. Several of the plane people set up a scholarship fund for local students to which over two million dollars has been donated. What this strange and wonderful incident left behind is a stunning example of kindness and generosity, but also something else: The human desire to connect with others, and the incredible power of such connections.[1]

The Power of Real Connection

Healthy leaders create emotional bonds with their teams, like the citizens of Gander did with their guests. We are wired to seek connections in our world. Humans are social creatures by design—and healthy leaders know and prioritize this truth. They excel not only at connecting directly with their team members, but also at helping team members connect with one another—in healthy ways. We often hear people speak with envy about companies like Starbucks, Ben & Jerry's, Southwest Airlines, Harley-Davidson, Nordstrom, The Container Store, and FedEx, to name a few. Outsiders are constantly looking for secrets to success in these companies. One "secret" is their culture of connectedness. They intentionally create strong connections to meaning, to team, and to contributions that fulfill the human needs of purpose, belonging, and appreciation.

To illustrate the power of connections, consider an experiment conducted to study the effects of relationships on group performance. The researchers compared the performance of groups of three friends to groups of three acquaintances. Each group was asked to follow specific instructions for building models made with Tinkertoy® pieces. The friends built an average of 9.0 models versus 2.45 models for the acquaintances. "The friends were able to challenge one another's ideas in a constructive way," said Karen Jehn, one of the researchers. "In the groups of acquaintances, people were almost too polite."[2]

One of the fastest ways to connect with others is to find common ground. This is true whether you are building a new relationship or building a bridge to mend an existing one. Consider two people who are at odds and walk away from negotiations as a lost cause. Then in walks a skilled mediator who quickly identifies a win-win solution. The contentious parties were focusing on differences while the mediator focused on commonalities.

So, what is the lesson here? Connections among teammates increase team health as measured by engagement and productivity. Sure, digital connectivity greases the wheels of high performance, but emotional connection is the engine. Another compelling study demonstrates that a feeling of connection can alter how our brains process the challenges we face. Researchers found that if a person is looking at a hill and judging how steep it is, the simple presence of a social support (like a friend) made the hill look 10 to 20 percent less steep than if the individual were alone. You or your team's perception of a task, goal, or project is transformed for the better when the presence of others is felt on the journey to achievement.[3] A healthy leader makes sure his or her team is looking up that hill, not alone but together.

Here's how you can build ties between your team's work and three emotional needs: purpose, belonging, and appreciation.

Connect to Meaning to Fulfill the Need for Purpose

Healthy leaders are bridge builders. One important bridge they build is between a team member's work and a bigger purpose. There are two levels of purpose that leaders connect employees to: organizational purpose and team purpose. Organizational purpose relates to making the world a better place or improving the human condition through work.

For instance, one of our clients distributes products to homebuilders. Their purpose did not seem very inspiring to the leadership team or to employees, yet a deeper look revealed a purpose worth connecting to: This company was a key link in the distribution chain, getting raw building products to sites where homes were being built for first-time home buyers. In essence, this company realized that they helped make the American dream of homeownership a reality. This new, more profound sense of purpose sparked a stronger sense of connection.

An organization's purpose can come in a variety of forms. Perhaps it is to create a sustainable product, to make the world a better place, or to innovate the best products to ease peoples' lives. Coca-Cola employees work diligently to achieve the company's purpose: "to refresh the world and make a difference." Google's mission is "to organize the world's information and make it universally accessible and useful." Southwest Airlines' purpose is "to connect people to what's important in their lives through friendly, reliable, and low-cost air travel." McDonald's purpose is "to be our customers' favorite place and way to eat and drink." Nordstrom aims "to give customers the most compelling shopping experience possible." All these companies connect business to purpose, and they connect purpose to employees' roles.

Your Team's Compelling Purpose

Cheryl Johnson was a client of ours when she was a leader at Fossil, a watch manufacturer and lifestyle brand, and then at Ulta Beauty. Now she is chief human resources officer for Paylocity. A discussion Lee had with her illustrates the importance of team purpose. They talked about how connecting to meaningful work ignites a personal passion to go the extra mile. Cheryl was reflecting on one of her first jobs during college—as a dishwasher in a hospital. Interestingly, she didn't see her job as that of only a dishwasher. Most people would wallow in the mundane task of washing dishes, but Cheryl's boss painted a picture of something much more significant. On the first day of work, he told Cheryl that her department's purpose was "to help ensure a clean, healthy environment so patients could heal as fast as possible and go home to their families." And it was Cheryl's role to contribute to that purpose by keeping the dishes clean. Wouldn't you be more passionate about washing dishes if that was *your* purpose?

No matter how large or small your team, healthy leaders define a compelling purpose for their teams. The most important motivational question a leader can answer for his/her team is, "Why am I doing this?" Sometimes articulating the answer is difficult because it requires a deep look at your business. For example, at one customer call center, the purpose is to provide a fair solution and brighten the day of every caller.

A technology department's purpose is to improve personal productivity. No matter what it is, a compelling purpose must create positive meaning in employees' lives.

You must also keep your compelling purpose real and relevant, since people can commit only to what they understand. A purpose is your team's bridge to a brighter, more connected tomorrow. Healthy leaders build bridges between each job and the team's purpose. Before you spring into action, keep in mind that a project goal is not the same as a purpose. Neither is a financial target nor a strategic plan. Most (non-sales) employees will not get emotionally charged up about a 10 percent net profit, a 20 percent return on investment, or a 30 percent increase in market share. A true purpose is a reason to be excited about getting up and going to work every day.

Involve Your Team

As a leader, it's powerful to involve your team to help define or refine the purpose. And you can bet, if your team is part of the process, they will be more engaged and committed. Work with them to answer these questions:

Why do we exist as a team? Since people tend to respond with what they do—their function—rather than *why* they do it, keep asking why, why, why? This will help reveal the core purpose of their work.

How does our team's purpose make you feel? If you hear responses like "proud," "important," "connected," "helpful," or "like a winner," then you're on the right track. If not, then ask, "What is missing?" or "What is a purpose that would make you feel excited?"

Does our purpose make you look at your job differently? What can you change or do differently to better support our purpose?

Discussions about these questions will help your team work more purposefully. Today's worker is more focused on purpose than ever, so engage them to find meaning in their work and in your team.

It's not enough to be busy. So are the ants.
The question is: What are we busy about?
—HENRY DAVID THOREAU,
American poet and philosopher

Connect to Team to Fulfill the Need for Belonging

Next fall, when you see geese heading south for the winter, flying along in V formation, you might consider what science has discovered about why they fly that way. As each bird flaps its wings, it creates an uplift for the bird immediately following. By flying in V formation, the whole flock adds at least 71 percent greater flying range than it would have if each bird flew alone. When a goose falls out of formation, it suddenly feels the drag and resistance of trying to go it alone and quickly falls back into formation to take advantage of the lifting power of the bird in front of it. And when the head goose gets tired, it rotates back in the formation, and another goose flies in the lead position.

People are remarkably like geese. When we share common goals and a sense of community, we can get where we are going more quickly and easily because we are traveling with the support of those around us. Likewise, it is sensible to take turns doing demanding jobs the way geese do. These birds also honk from behind to encourage those up front to keep up their speed. We all need encouragement along life's journey, whether it's a pat on the back or an appreciative email (but probably not a honk). Finally, when a goose gets sick or is wounded by a gunshot and falls out of formation, two other geese fall out with that goose and follow it down to lend help and protection. They stay with the fallen goose until it is able to fly or until it dies; and only then do they launch out on their own or join another formation to catch up with their group. It's up to a healthy leader to create this geese-like sense of belonging and shared direction.

We long to belong. So, success is rarely achieved alone. It is almost always achieved with the help of others along the way. If we use the approach of the goose, we will make progress alongside one another. Geese are defined by how they stay connected to one another. Healthy leaders and their teams are defined the same way.

Rituals Connect Us

Back in your childhood, you may have belonged to a club that had a secret handshake. Just knowing that handshake made you feel like you were a part of the group, right? It was a "belonging" factor that made you feel connected. The handshake was something special that only members could do or know. In your work life, feeling like part of a team provides that same sense of belonging. When this need goes unmet, however, you feel alone and disconnected. If you don't feel connected to others, you come to work each day, but you leave your heart at home.

Rituals make members feel connected to one another through unique yet common experiences. As a result, they create strong and long-lasting personal connections that are group specific. Now, before you think we are suggesting that you start teaching secret handshakes at onboardings for new employees, let us translate the practice of rituals into the business setting. Every team has rituals, regardless of whether you recognize them as such. Organizations have rituals around hiring, recognition, production, innovation, quality, promotions, family, customer service, community service, learning, and numerous other practices. To be clear, we are not advocating rituals for ritual's sake. They should be intentionally designed to meet a business need or the team's need for connection. Healthy rituals fit your leadership style and the chemistry of your team—they feel natural. And they are performed with 100 percent reliability. If you celebrate team members' birthdays monthly on "Last Friday Birthdays," but you forgot to do it twice last year, then it's not a ritual. Healthy rituals are reliable and positively anticipated by teams. Here are a few ways you can use team rituals to enhance a sense of belonging:

What do you want to reinforce?	Which rituals fit your leadership style and team culture?
Outstanding performance	• "Ring the bell" to announce success! • Pass a fun trophy to someone who has gone above and beyond (should be public and ceremonial). • Take the "star" to lunch. Use a simple cardboard star as a symbol of outstanding performance; present it to the recipient, then take him/her to lunch.
Productive relationships/ teamwork	• Begin with morning huddles to identify your focus for the day (yes, regular meetings are a ritual). • Assign "buddies" to new team members. • Host Last Friday Brown Bag Lunches or First Monday Donut/Bagel Days, whether in-person or virtually. • Make the rounds each morning to say "hello" to your team (walk around or call around).
Community service	• Organize a relay team for an annual weekend walk/run to support a local charity. • Package or serve meals as a team at a local food bank once a quarter. • As a team, tutor children at a local school on a regular basis.

To be intentional about your team rituals, start with a specific team need, and then determine if you already have a ritual in place that reinforces that need. If not, create one. For example, at one client, the sales and marketing departments were very siloed and not communicating about important prospecting data. To resolve this, the manager started a Taco Tuesday lunch where both the sales and marketing teams ran through the prospect list and their respective plans to garner the new business, aiding in collaboration and coordination between departments. Not only did members of each team get to know each other and work better together, but they were able to close more sales.

Rituals that are well designed stand the test of time; even so, occasionally a ritual can become "stale" or it no longer reinforces the need. In that case, change up the elements that aren't working or replace the ritual with a new one. If you do not have a ritual in place, get creative and develop one that feels fresh and organic. Then systematize it so it's easy to sustain. Finally, make sure to involve your team in this process—they are often the best source of ideas for rituals.

Connect to Contributions to Fulfill the Need for Appreciation

Charles Plumb was a U.S. Naval Academy graduate, one of the original Top Gun pilots, and a pilot in Vietnam. On May 19, 1967, during his 75th combat mission (five days before the end of his tour), his plane was shot down. He ejected and parachuted into enemy hands, where he spent six years in a Vietnamese prison. He survived the ordeal and now speaks to share his lessons learned from that experience.

One day, Plumb and his wife were sitting in a restaurant when a man came up and said, "You're Plumb! You flew jet fighters in Vietnam from the aircraft carrier Kitty Hawk. You were shot down!"

"How in the world did you know that?" Plumb asked cautiously and curiously.

"I packed your parachute," the man replied. Plumb gasped in surprise and gratitude. The man pumped his hand and said, "I guess it worked!"

Plumb assured him, "It sure did. If that chute hadn't worked, I wouldn't be here today."

That night, thinking about the man, Plumb couldn't sleep. He thought of the many hours the sailor had spent on a long wooden table in the bowels of the ship, carefully folding the silks of each chute, holding someone's fate in his hands.

Plumb later said, "I kept wondering what he might have looked like in a Navy uniform—white hat, bib in the back, bell-bottom trousers. I wondered how many times I might have seen him and not even said, "Good morning, how are you?" because, you see, I was a fighter pilot, and he was *just* a sailor."

We all have someone who supports our success the way that sailor ensured Plumb's survival. Focus on each person and their individual contributions, not their titles. Remember, at the end of the day, your success is based more on what your people do than on what you do.

So, who's packing *your* parachute, and are you making them feel appreciated?

Big Value, No Cost

People want to feel valued for their work. In fact, lack of appreciation is a key reason people leave jobs. Showing appreciation is a common blind spot for leaders—and for people in any relationship, for that matter. You no doubt feel appreciative of your team; yet, it's highly likely there's a gap between how much your team feels appreciated and how much you really appreciate them. Why is that? This disconnect exists because people typically do not convert every thought of appreciation into words and actions. While we judge ourselves by our intentions, others judge us by our actions. What is important is not how much you *think* you appreciate your team's contributions, but rather how much you *demonstrate* your appreciation. The ultimate goal is that your team feels seen, valued, and recognized.

A survey of 15 million people worldwide illuminates the business benefits of appreciation. This Gallup study by Tom Rath and Donald O. Clifton found that people who receive regular recognition at work displayed a host of positive behaviors such as:

- Heightened productivity;

- Increased engagement with colleagues;

- Greater likelihood of staying with the organization;

- Higher loyalty and satisfaction scores from customers; and,

- Better safety records and fewer accidents on the job.[4]

Appreciation comes down to basic psychology. It feels good, so we do more of what we are appreciated for, and this increases motivation. As a leader, first reinforce those behaviors that you want to see more frequently. Next, look for opportunities to recognize and appreciate your team's efforts and results. Finally, catch your employees doing something right . . . and encourage them to do it often. Research from Gallup revealed that the most effective teams have at least a 3:1 ratio of positive to negative interactions. Demonstrating appreciation for contributions is a powerful way to create a positive interaction. On the home front, this same research found the ratio for the most effective marriages is at least 5:1. Bottom line: It is wise to apply this ratio for your home team and your work team.

When it comes to demonstrating appreciation, you have complete control. No budget limitations or excuses here—there are literally thousands of ways to demonstrate your appreciation at little to no cost. You can occasionally offer a gift card or some other token of modest value, but you should rely more on your creativity and knowledge of the employee to personalize the gesture. The key to demonstrating your appreciation is making it sincere, specific, and meaningful. Don't fall into the trap of blurting out the robotic, "Good job." Take time to explain why you appreciate an employee's performance, such as, "I really appreciate the way you kept our customer happy without incurring additional cost."

In our work at client organizations, we have seen more than a few handwritten notes of appreciation on employees' desks. Often these cards are several years old (five-plus years in several cases), yet they are still prominently and proudly displayed. That speaks volumes about emotional connection. We often wonder if the bosses who wrote them understand how much discretionary effort their three-minute investment yielded or know how meaningful those cards were to those employees. Greg Brown, chief customer service officer at Blue Cross and Blue Shield of Illinois, Montana, New Mexico, Oklahoma, and Texas, says, "The little things you do are more important than the big things you say." He sends electronic anniversary cards to each of his 1,000-plus leaders. He also makes a habit of writing notes to anyone he catches doing something right.[5] Find a way to express your appreciation that is natural to you. Not everyone is a note-card writer, but every leader can find a way to demonstrate appreciation that feels authentic.

Appreciate Progress

We often hear leaders say that they will appreciate their teams once a certain goal is achieved. These leaders do not understand the power of appreciating progress. Healthy leaders appreciate results *and* progress. They understand that employees want to feel connected to their leader, their organization, and their purpose—not just after the final buzzer when the team wins, but throughout the game.

Let's say a team member has a sales goal of closing ten deals by the end of the quarter. If you wait until the end of the quarter to discuss the employee's performance, you will have missed the opportunity to positively encourage their progress along the way. But if you notice a team member made the targeted fifty calls today, you can recognize this progress and increase the probability that this employee will make the targeted number of calls the next day. By the same token, if your team member makes only twenty-five calls in a day, you have an opportunity to encourage him or her and explain how the current call volume directly affects the team's results.

There are different ways to create a feeling of connection among your team—through purpose, belonging, and appreciation. Healthy leaders know how to activate pathways of real connection so that everyone reaps the benefits. People do more for those who appreciate them, and they do more of the behavior that is appreciated. This is a powerful human dynamic that healthy leaders know how to leverage.

The way to develop the best that is in a person
is by appreciation and encouragement.
—CHARLES SCHWAB,
American investor and financial executive

Cultivate Healthy Leadership

CONNECT
Build ties between work and human needs

✓ Connect to meaning by asking my team these questions about our purpose:
- Why does our team exist?
- Does our purpose make you look at your job differently?
- What can you change or do differently to better support our purpose?

✓ Connect to team with rituals that fulfill the need for belonging:
- Meet a specific need.
- Feel authentic to my leadership style.
- Perform with 100 percent reliability.

✓ Connect to contributions to make my team feel appreciated:
- Ensure at least a 3:1 ratio of positive to negative interactions.
- Be specific in my expressions of appreciation.
- Acknowledge progress as well as results.

My commitment to **Connect**:

_____

_____

_____

*Communication—the human connection—
is the key to personal and career success.*

—PAUL J. MEYER,
pioneer of self-improvement

7

COACH
Unlock the potential in others

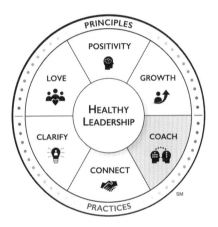

We love the Olympics. In fact, we were thrilled when they started alternating the summer and winter Olympics so that we would only have to wait two years instead of four to watch the games. The Olympics embody all that is good and inspiring about the human spirit. We are in awe of how these athletes practice day in and day out, week in and week out, year in and year out, for that one moment to perform when it really matters.

As we watched the most recent Olympics, we had an aha moment. Olympians spend 99 percent of their time practicing, while they perform just 1 percent (or less) of the time. Your team members have the opposite challenge. They must perform 99 percent (or more) of the time—taking care of customers, analyzing reports, developing their teams, generating sales, and meeting other organizational needs. In business, there is precious little time for your team to "practice" all these tasks that keep the company running. The vast majority of your team's learning and development happens on the job rather than in formal training programs.

Those who coach Olympic athletes literally spend years training their athletes and typically can only sit and watch as they perform. Leaders in a work setting, on the other hand, have the chance to coach their team members day in and day out, for years, in real time, as they perform. That is a powerful distinction, and it creates a special opportunity for healthy leaders to help their teams flourish.

Even though we are hardly Olympic athletes ourselves, we have experienced the power of a coach to elevate performance in real time when we exercise (Pilates for Julie and TITLE® Boxing for Lee). The moment the trainer or coach is within eyesight, we predictably increase our intensity, exert more energy, and check to ensure our form is correct. This natural human reaction to work harder when being observed (or encouraged) has long been established. In fact, the first study to demonstrate this effect was conducted by Norman Triplett, a psychologist from Indiana University, way back in 1898.[1] The fact that we perform better when we are coached in real time is referred to as *social facilitation*, which is defined as "an improvement in performance produced by the mere presence of others."

Ally or Critic?

Do you coach your team in real-time? What are the possibilities for offering feedback, adjusting on the fly, tweaking execution, changing plans mid-game if needed, and encouraging them? Not only does your team deserve a leader to help them realize their full potential, but Gallup's research (discussed in Chapter 1) also reveals that your team wants a coach, not a boss. They want a coach who helps them grow and develop personally and professionally. Yet to coach your team in healthy ways, you must first ensure you have a healthy mindset. The key to a healthy coaching mindset is to be the employee's ally, not the critic.

If we asked a room of 1,000 people to speak up if they like being criticized, we would hear crickets. Why? Because critics think they know better than you and stunt your openness to grow. Criticism is predictably met with resistance and yields modest, short-term change at best. On the contrary, when you are seen as an ally, employees know you care about their well-being and success, and they feel your confidence and commitment to help them grow. The bottom line: Healthy leaders are allies for their teams and they coach from that position.[2]

Darren Woodson was a strong, star safety for the Dallas Cowboys for thirteen years, a three-time Super Bowl Champion, and a five-time Pro Bowl selection. He followed his celebrated NFL career as an ESPN analyst for thirteen years after that. Today, he is a partner at Cresa, a leading commercial real estate services company. At an event we hosted, Darren graciously agreed to kick off the session and address the CEOs in attendance. After telling several captivating stories, he recalled the five NFL coaches he played under. One of them was Bill Parcells, who had a reputation of being a tough coach. Surprisingly, Darren shared that below Coach Parcells' hard, gruff exterior, he deeply and genuinely cared for his players as people. He would even intentionally connect with them off the field.[3] Coach Parcells helped Darren see that the best coaches want to help make team members into better people, and healthy leaders do the same.

A healthy coaching mindset assumes the best intent, looks for what is good, seeks first to understand, and trusts others' capabilities. This enables the leader to focus on strengths, coach with questions, and help employees move toward autonomy. Now, let's discuss how.

Focus on Strengths to Achieve Mastery

Most types of sports equipment—a golf club, a tennis racket, a baseball bat—have a certain spot that, if the ball hits it, will give the player the optimal result. Hitting this sweet spot yields a long drive down the fairway, a swift crosscourt return, or a home-run swing. If you have experienced it, you know that when you hit the sweet spot, you barely feel it. The ball goes exactly where you want it to go—even farther and faster than you'd imagined. Doesn't get any better than that!

As a healthy leader, you have a huge opportunity to help your employees find their professional sweet spots. This ensures the "highest and best use" of their talents. Wouldn't you love having every team member working in his or her sweet spot and being perfectly fitted to their jobs? They would more often get into "the zone," and work would feel like play. Coach your team members to find their sweet spots by asking two simple questions:

1. **What are you passionate about?**
   (e.g., company culture, our industry, community service, new technology, connecting people, solving problems, the environment, generating wealth, family, sports, arts, product design, consumer psychology, etc.)

2. **Which tasks are very easy and natural for you to perform?**
   (e.g., analyzing data, managing people, coordinating projects, improving processes, creative design, serving clients, selling, team building, delivering presentations, etc.)

Most of us vividly remember the moment we found our professional sweet spot. Was there an instance when someone told you that you made it look easy, that you really excelled, that you looked like you were having a blast? Think of a time when you were at your best and others made comments like these. What were you doing? Help your team members find the intersection between their answers to these questions and the roles and tasks at hand—that's their sweet spot. Discuss these questions with your employees to help them find a place of mastery that will serve them and your team well.

A Sweet-spot Story

Oftentimes, cultivating talent isn't a linear path—it zigs and zags. As part of your role in helping your employees find their sweet spots, you need to structure their wanderings with a sense of direction. This was true of Tony Robbins. Most people know him as a self-help author, speaker, and philanthropist who has transformed millions of peoples' lives. But before Robbins became arguably the world's most famous life coach, he was a teenager from a difficult family situation in need of coaching himself. He had no idea where his talents lay, though he was extremely motivated to find a purpose in life and make a difference—he just didn't know how to go about doing this. Fortunately, he found guidance in the form of a man named Jim Rohn, an entrepreneur and pioneer in the field of motivational seminars, who started coaching Robbins.

As an ambitious and energetic young man, Robbins wanted to have an impact—and *fast*. Rohn convinced him to slow down, stop focusing on outcomes and instead start focusing on strengthening his skills. You can't put success before having a talent in place first. Robbins listened, while also heeding Rohn's advice to look for his value and consider how he could help others. Additionally, he adopted Rohn's recommendation to read every single day in search of new insights and inspiration. This approach paid off for Robbins. Thanks to Rohn's coaching, he combined his interests in behavioral science with his own brand of high-intensity, high-connection motivational speaking. He created a powerful new style of coaching that drew more and more people to him, eager to hear what he had to say.[4]

By his mid-20s, Robbins had a best-selling book, a blossoming career and, most importantly, a deep knowledge of his passion and strengths: he'd found his sweet spot. In a tribute to Rohn soon after his death, Robbins recalled, "He gave me a way of looking at life that allowed me to not ask life to be easier, but to ask that I be better. He got me to realize that the secret to life was to work harder on myself than my job or anything else, because then I'd have something to give people."[5]

Rohn helped Robbins find his competence, and competence builds confidence. It makes sense: The quickest way to build competence is to start with strengths. In fact, a study by the Corporate Leadership Council that included 19,187 employees from thirty-four countries across seven industries, using standardized measures of individual performance, found that managers who used a strength-based approach with their employees helped improve performance by 36.4 percent. On the other hand, managers who focused primarily on employees' weaknesses saw employees' performance decrease by 26.8 percent.[6] So, shift your focus from what is wrong to what is strong.

If you are committed to healthy results and relationships, then focus on strengths when you coach your team. Lead them to their sweet spots by looking for their natural gifts and helping them thrive in those areas.

Our job as leaders is not to put in what God left out but to draw out what God left in.
—MARCUS BUCKINGHAM,
from *First, Break All the Rules*

Coach with Questions to Facilitate Engagement

A few summers ago, we enjoyed a family trip to Greece. It is a land of boundless beauty with a long history of tremendous thinkers. While touring the Acropolis of Athens, our guide mentioned that when the restoration of this prized structure was being scheduled, time was budgeted for each worker to spend time thinking! Imagine that happening almost anywhere else in the world, but since Greece's history is built upon the minds of the world's greatest thinkers, it makes sense.

One of those great thinkers is the philosopher Socrates, who was born more than 2,500 years ago. Today, he is alive and well in any coach who inspires others to realize their potential. His Socratic method of questioning is a timely and timeless leadership tool for engaging teams and challenging thought processes. Asking questions serves the needs of your employees and also serves the needs of the leader. It demonstrates interest in your team while providing you with insights into their motivations, passions, challenges, assumptions, and aspirations. The next time you are tempted to tell your team what to do, take a lesson from Socrates and ask for their perspectives first.

Questions Are the Answer

When it comes to coaching, questions are actually the answer. By simply asking questions, your employees will reveal challenges and opportunities that could potentially take you months or even years to identify. Remember, we all want to be seen and heard, and asking questions meets that need.

Asking questions and then really listening demonstrates personal respect and a genuine desire to engage and develop your team. Listen for the entire message your employee is communicating with his or her words, tone, posture, eyes, energy, hesitations, fluency, etc. Healthy leaders listen at least 50 percent of the time. Our client Andrew Levi, an excellent leader of numerous successful businesses, has done a tremendous amount of presenting and explaining in his efforts to build healthy cultures and businesses. On the topic of listening, he says, "He who talks the most loses."[7]

Ask, be silent, and listen to engage your team. What you discover will help you be a better coach. Healthy leaders make concerted efforts to keep in touch with the realities of their employees. They listen for the truth, even if it turns out to be uncomfortable or inconvenient. Ask your employees what they think and listen to their answers. But what questions should you ask? Certain coaching questions work in almost any situation. These are five of our favorites to engage your team members:

- What do you think?

- Why do you think this is happening?

- What can we start, stop, and keep doing, to improve our work?

- And what else? (Repeated as a prompt to obtain more details.)

- Is this your very best work? (Lee's mentor asks him this question.)

There is rarely a right answer to a wrong question. Asking questions without a clear objective is like playing the question lotto. Occasionally you might get lucky and win, but most of the time you will come up empty-handed. That's a loss for you and for your team member.

There are four main reasons to ask questions: to understand, to assess, to innovate, and to motivate. It is important to know your objectives before you start asking. Within each objective, your question might focus on the person or the project/process. The following table serves as a guide to keep your coaching questions purposeful.

UNDERSTAND	ASSESS	INNOVATE	MOTIVATE
To gain knowledge and solicit insights	To determine options and make decisions	To generate ideas and improve methods	To achieve a goal and implement a plan
The Person • In which areas would you like to grow? • What do you love to do? • What do you need to be at your very best? • What would you like to be doing in three years? • How can we more fully utilize your skills? • What are you really passionate about? • What's your "why," your core motivation for working?	**The Person** • What would you change if you were in my position? • What's the most important thing you can accomplish today? • Which option makes the most sense to you? • What are the consequences of the choices? • What does your gut tell you? • What one thing could you improve to elevate your game?	**The Person** • What would you do if funds were unlimited? • What would you do differently if you had no fear of failing? • When do you feel the most creative? • Who do you brainstorm the best with? • What's one thing you would change today? • What do you think our business will look like in 10 years?	**The Person** • What needs to happen for this to succeed? • What do you think the next steps should be? • What's in it for you and the team if this is wildly successful? • How can I best help or support you? • How can we maintain focus and excitement? • Do we have the right people in the right roles to ensure success?
The Project / Process • What's the goal? • What is your plan? • What are the alternative choices being considered? • What's the current situation? • What would you need to make this project succeed? • Who are the key players on your team? • Who are the stakeholders?	**The Project / Process** • What is your next step? • What conclusions have you reached so far? • What's the biggest risk? • What are the key factors in making this decision? • What is conflicting with your most important priorities? • How can we collect 80% of the data we need in the shortest time possible?	**The Project / Process** • What if we looked at this from a totally different perspective? • How could we do this in half the time? • Who does this process better than anyone in the world? • Which steps do not add value to our customer? • What is one more alternative to consider?	**The Project / Process** • What barriers do you need removed? • How will we know if we are successful? • What are the key milestones we must hit to stay on track? • What are a few quick wins we can achieve and celebrate? • What is the accountability process? • What's going well so far?

It is not the answer that enlightens, but the question.

—EUGENE IONESCO,
Romanian-French playwright

Coach Toward Autonomy to Inspire Ownership

Jeff Immelt is former CEO of General Electric and a three-time recipient of *Barron's* "World's Best CEO." One of Immelt's leadership tips is: Manage by setting boundaries, with freedom in the middle (in other words, give your employees autonomy). He says, "The boundaries are commitment, passion, trust, and teamwork. Within those boundaries, there's plenty of freedom."[8] As intuitive as Immelt's advice might appear in theory, giving employees autonomy is not always intuitive or comfortable for leaders in practice. Control leads to compliant behavior, but autonomy inspires ownership behavior. Giving autonomy is generally more important than doing it "the way the boss said to do it." What's the risk of not providing autonomy? Employees basically become robots—they give you their hands and feet, but not their minds and hearts. Healthy leaders realize there is more than one way to effectively solve a problem, more than one way to approach a job, and more than one way to achieve results. An employee's approach might be different than the leader's approach, but the benefits of their ownership in the work far outweigh any loss of control that leaders might feel.

Job autonomy has accelerated as remote work has become more the norm. However, working remotely, in and of itself, does not fulfill the need for autonomy. Clarity is a key enabler for coaching toward autonomy. Regardless of where work is performed, remotely or in the office, unclear vision, values, and expectations inhibit an employee's ability to work autonomously. For example, when we coach CEOs on challenges with their team's autonomy, very frequently the problem lies in the lack of clear and consistently communicated vision, values, and expectations. Once the leader and team members clarify and align on vision, values, and expectations (as we discussed in Chapter 5), they create a clear context for working more autonomously and for being successful. This clear context enables team members to choose how to perform the job within the agreed-upon context. Ultimately this results in ownership behavior by team members giving their discretionary time and effort to achieve team goals. This is the holy grail for any leader. So, here's the coaching for autonomy equation: **Clarity + Autonomy = Ownership Behavior.**

To coach for autonomy, anchor your coaching discussions on your team's vision, values, and expectations. Discuss with team members how their performance is aligned or misaligned with the agreed-upon expectations. Of course, you must ensure you are providing the necessary resources, information, and access for them to be successful. Then, focus on results. If results are falling short, shift the focus of the coaching discussion from work results to work process—what they can do differently or more consistently to meet expectations. For example, if a salesperson is performing well, you appreciate the results and ask how they can be sustained through next quarter. On the other hand, if a salesperson is not delivering the expected results, it is appropriate to explore the work process. Is s/he qualifying leads effectively, making the expected number of sales calls, and following up consistently? Your goal is not to micromanage, but rather to identify a solution that enables this salesperson to succeed and grow into more autonomy.

When you give team members autonomy, they own their results. What's the benefit to you and the team you lead? People support what they help create. When you give discretion to your team on how to do their work, you get their discretionary effort. That is, employees willingly give their time and energy to help achieve team goals.

What's the Small Idea?

Leaders at Toyota coach toward autonomy to build ownership behavior in their teams. As part of The Toyota Way, employees submit suggestions to their team. They are suggestions the employees can implement themselves or with a teammate—in other words, this initiative is something employees control without need for management approval.

At one point, Toyota received about 1.5 million employee improvement ideas each year. More impressively, 80 percent of these ideas were implemented, saving the company $300 million annually. Keep in mind, these are frontline manufacturing workers whom you might think typically have less autonomy than an office worker. These impressive results required no executive approval or committees. That's autonomy at work! So, how did Toyota do it?

Virtually all these ideas are implemented at the employee level. Executives don't oversee how the suggestions get addressed. Problems and improvements are identified, solved, and measured by each team—the experts in their jobs. It's not the company mandating these improvements; rather, accountability and results are driven at the ground level, where the rubber meets the road.

Even though many of Toyota's employees perform repetitive jobs in auto assembly plants, they are empowered to be thoughtful and engaged about improving their work output and their work lives. This approach sends a strong message that employees have control. It's no surprise that Toyota became America's top automaker in 2021. This is the first time a non-domestic automaker has taken the top spot in America.[9]

This growth in the deeply entrenched U.S. auto market was powered by a healthy need for autonomy. What kind of impact would this approach to autonomy have in your organization?

Being a great coach means many things. It is about unlocking the potential in others by helping employees cultivate their strengths, asking the right questions, and providing autonomy so employees take ownership for results.

Cultivate Healthy Leadership

COACH
Unlock the potential in others

✓ Focus on strengths to achieve mastery:
- Ask my team members what they are passionate about, and which tasks come naturally to them.
- Shift my focus from what is wrong to what is strong.

✓ Coach with questions to facilitate engagement:
- Ask purposeful questions to understand, assess, innovate, or motivate.
- Listen at least 50 percent of the time.

✓ Coach toward autonomy to inspire ownership:
- Anchor my coaching discussions on my team's vision, values, and expectations.
- If results are falling short, shift my focus from outputs (results) to inputs (process) to identify what my team member can do differently to meet expectations.

My commitment to **Coach**:

_____

_____

_____

A coach is someone who tells you what you don't want to hear, who has you see what you don't want to see, so you can be who you always knew you could be.

—TOM LANDRY, former Dallas Cowboys head coach

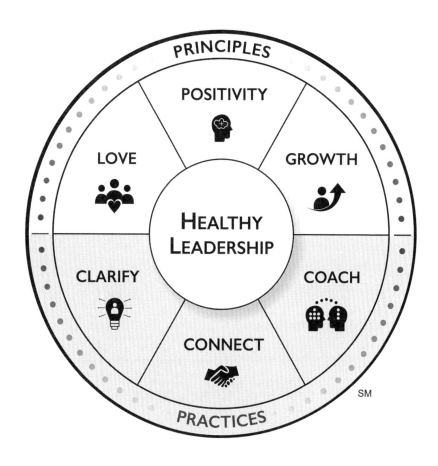

Healthy Leadership At-a-Glance

PRINCIPLES

Love: *Do what is in the best interest of others.*
- Put the team before me.
- Be human. See the human.
- Respect people and perspectives.

Positivity: *Manage negative emotions and increase positive ones.*
- Manage your mind.
- Talk yourself up.
- Encourage others.

Growth: *Seek new insights, knowledge, and skills.*
- Become an expert on you.
- Cultivate curiosity.
- Learn from adversity.

PRACTICES

Clarify: *Crystalize a desired future and motivation to get there.*
- Clarify vision to inspire action.
- Clarify values to guide behaviors and decisions.
- Clarify expectations to execute with excellence.

Connect: *Build ties between work and human needs.*
- Connect to meaning to fulfill the need for purpose.
- Connect to team to fulfill the need for belonging.
- Connect to contributions to fulfill the need for appreciation.

Coach: *Unlock the potential in others.*
- Coach on strengths to achieve mastery.
- Coach with questions to facilitate engagement.
- Coach toward autonomy to inspire ownership.

Take this two-minute Healthy Leadership assessment, then receive a real-time feedback report. theLgroup.com/healthy-leadership-checkup

8

Leading the Way

Two young men were working their way through Stanford University in the late 1890s when, during one semester, their funds got desperately low. They came up with a plan: They would invite Ignacy Paderewski, the great Polish pianist, to give a performance. After paying the concert expenses, the two students would then use the profits from ticket sales to pay their room, board, and tuition.

The pianist's manager asked for a guarantee of two thousand dollars. Undaunted, the students accepted the terms and staged the concert. Alas, the concert generated only sixteen hundred dollars total—not enough to even pay Paderewski. The big gamble was a bust. After the performance, the students sought the famous pianist, gave him the entire sixteen hundred dollars, a promissory note for four hundred dollars, and explained they would earn the remainder of his fee and send the money to him.

"No," replied Paderewski, "that won't do." Then tearing the note to shreds, he returned the money and said to the two young men. "Now, take out of these sixteen hundred dollars all of your expenses and keep for each of you 10 percent of the balance for your work."

The students happily accepted this act of generosity.

The years rolled by—years of fortune and destiny. Paderewski became the Prime Minister of Poland. The devastation of World War I came, and Paderewski's only focus was to feed the starving thousands in his beloved country, but this seemed an impossible task. Yet, just as the need was most severe, thousands of tons of food began to arrive in Poland for distribution. It turned out the supplies had come from the United States—from the American Relief Administration.

After all the starving people were fed and hard times had passed, Paderewski journeyed to Paris to thank the head of the American Relief Administration for the food he had sent. That man would soon become the President of the United States. His name was Herbert Hoover.

"That's all right, Mr. Paderewski," said Mr. Hoover upon meeting the Polish leader. "You don't remember it, but you helped me once when I was a student at college, and I was in a hole. You invested in me . . . now it's my turn."

Investing in other people is a wise strategy for leaders. It provides a far greater return on investment than the best mutual fund—and the dividends can manifest in unexpected ways, as they did for Paderewski. Your investment in future leaders is the best predictor of healthy growth for your team and your business. Healthy leaders inspire good employees to become even better people. They help others build better lives for themselves.

If you continually give, you will continually have.
—Chinese proverb

Team Care Starts with Self-care

Can you recite the flight attendant's safety speech? We bet you can. You know, the one that goes something like, ". . . In the event of a loss of cabin pressure, an oxygen mask will drop from above. If you are traveling with a child, place your mask on first . . .." We found this version of the safety speech written by a flight attendant who was trying to break the monotony and win the attention of the passengers:

> *In the event of a loss of cabin pressure, these baggy things will drop down over your head. You stick it over your nose and mouth like the flight attendant is doing now. The bag won't inflate, but there's oxygen there, promise. If you are sitting next to a small child, or someone who is acting like a small child, please do us all a favor and put on your mask first. If you are traveling with two or more children, please take a moment now to decide which one is your favorite. Help that one first, and then work your way down.*

As a parent, it always seems counterintuitive to put your own mask on first (not to mention picking your favorite child!). The lesson in this speech for a healthy leader is simple: Take care of yourself, so you can better serve others. This sounds simple, but it can also feel unnatural for leaders accustomed to putting others' needs before their own. Failing to prioritize your own health can damage your ability to lead others.

If you are ever feeling the need for "oxygen" or that there is something a bit off that you can't quite put your finger on, think H.A.L.T. It's a simple reminder to take care of yourself and avoid getting too Hungry, Angry, Lonely, or Tired.

Hungry. Being hungry compromises your peak performance and focus. Keep your body appropriately fueled to minimize stress and maximize productivity. The more nutritious food your body gets and the fewer "empty calories" you consume, the happier your body becomes; this results in a healthier metabolism and less intense hunger signals. Also, avoid multitasking during snacks and meals. Your brain and five senses are an important part of digestion and satisfaction. If you eat while watching television or answering email, you won't really taste your food, which can lead your body to send out hunger signals even after you've eaten.

Angry. Remember that positive emotions expand possibilities you see, while negative emotions limit them. Unexpressed emotions do not go away, they just rear their heads in uglier ways. Carrying around anger will inevitably deteriorate relationships and your own body. The key is to vent your emotions in constructive ways: Talk feelings out with a trusted friend, write in your journal, use a creative outlet, exercise, meditate, or pray.

Lonely. Humans are fundamentally social creatures . . . yes, even those of you who are introverts. Don't misconstrue your social media friends for real interactions that make you feel connected, wanted, and cared for. Reach out to those at work, in your community, at your place of worship, from your alma mater—any place that feels comfortable for you. Choose to be present, to share words, laughter, and real-life connections.

Tired. If food is fuel for your body, then sleep is the pit crew providing needed maintenance. Sleep deprivation has been used as a form of wartime torture for good reason—it works. The average person requires seven hours of sleep per night to be at his/her best. Sleep replenishes. It serves as a cognitive car wash, restoring and refreshing your mind, body, and spirit. Take the long view and get the rest you need so you can sustain your productivity.

Healthy leaders are generally, well, *healthy*: They eat right, exercise, get regular checkups, read a lot, engage in hobbies, and have friends outside of work. It's what fuels their focus, creativity, and drive while they are on the job. Staying in balance physically, socially, spiritually, and emotionally, and recognizing the four H.A.L.T. triggers will help you stay at your best. Additionally, taking care of yourself sets a healthy example for your employees. If you care for yourself, then you'll be at your best to help your team be at its best . . . and thrive.

As you grow older, you will discover that you have two hands, one for helping yourself, the other for helping others.

—AUDREY HEPBURN,
British actress and humanitarian

Getting Started

As we mentioned earlier, we have great respect for Olympic athletes. They start with the right mindset, and they develop the habits necessary to achieve their goals. They also have a game plan when they step onto the court, ice, field, or track—specific strategies to put their training, both physical and mental, into action. The same holds true when it comes to cultivating healthy leadership. You can't just hope to succeed. You need a game plan.

The key to finishing big is to start small. Big achievements like running a marathon, introducing a new product, or exceeding a hefty sales goal all start with one small step. Consistent baby steps will get you to the finish line. Here are three easy steps to help you get started:

1. Take the complimentary, online Healthy Leadership checkup at: theLgroup.com/healthy-leadership-checkup

2. Use your assessment results to help select one of the personal commitments you wrote down at the end of Chapters 2-7. Identify small daily actions that will help you achieve the commitment you selected.

3. Share your personal commitment and your learnings from this book with your team so they can support you.

Congratulations on starting your journey toward healthy leadership by reading this book. Now, keep going and growing so everyone in your world of work will thrive, starting with you!

You don't have to be great to start,
but you have to start to be great.

—ZIG ZIGLAR,
American author and motivational speaker

Endnotes

Chapter 1: Leading in Today's World of Work

1. Thomas, A. (1988). Does leadership make a difference to organizational performance? *Administrative Science Quarterly*, 33(3), 388-400. Also, Cameron, K. S. (2012). *Positive Leadership: Strategies for extraordinary performance*. San Francisco, CA: Barrett-Koehler.

2. Thomas, A. (1988). Does leadership make a difference to organizational performance? *Administrative Science Quarterly*, 33(3), 388-400. Also, Liebersonb, S., & O'Connor, J. (1972). Leadership and organizational performance: A study of larger corporations. *American Sociological Review*, 37(2), 117-130. Also, Beck, R., & Harter, J. (2015, April 21). Managers account for 70% of variance in employee engagement. *Gallup Business Journal*. https://news.gallup.com/businessjounral/182792/managers-account-variance-employee-engagement.aspx

3. Gallup (2016). *How Millennials Want to Live and Work*, Gallup.

Chapter 2: Love

1. https://abcnews.go.com/US/ups-driver-special-christmas-residents-route/story?id=74888815

2. https://hbr.org/2016/01/manage-your-emotional-culture

3. https://leaderchat.org/2011/01/06/colleen-barrett-of-southwest-airlines-lead-with-luv/

4. Colleen Barrett, president emeritus, Southwest Airlines, personal interview, March 15, 2012.

5. https://www.youtube.com/watch?v=djoyd46TVVc

6. Fournies, F. (1999). *Why employees don't do what they're supposed to do . . . And what to do about it*. Liberty Hall Press.

7. Porath, C., George Washington University, TED Talk, *Why being respectful to your coworkers is good for business [Video]*. YouTube. https://youtu.be/YY1ERM-NIBY

Chapter 3: Positivity

1. https://www.linkedin.com/pulse/importance-teaching-mindset-schools-sara-blakely/

2. https://www.cnbc.com/2019/04/03/self-made-billionaire-spanx-founder-sara-blakely-sold-fax-machines-before-making-it-big.html

3. https://www.linkedin.com/pulse/importance-teaching-mindset-schools-sara-blakely/

4. Fredrickson, B. L. (2009). *Positivity: Discover the upward spiral that will change your life.* Harmony; 1st edition.

5. Cameron, K. (2021). *Positively energizing leadership.*, Berrett-Koehler,14-16.

6. Cameron, K. (2021). *Positively energizing leadership.*, Berrett-Koehler, 25.

7. Fredrickson, B. L., Cohn, M. A., Coffey, K. A., Pek, J., & Finkel, S. M. (2008). Open hearts build lives: Positive emotions, induced through loving-kindness meditation, build consequential personal resources. *Journal of Personality and Social Psychology*, 95(5), 1045-1062. https://www.ncbi.nlm.nih.gov/pmc/articles/PMC3156028/

8. Rock, D. (2009). *Your brain at work: Strategies for overcoming distraction, regaining focus, and working smarter all day long.* Harper Business, 1st edition.

9. Fredrickson, B. L., Cohn, M. A., Coffey, K. A., Pek, J., & Finkel, S. M. (2008). Open hearts build lives: Positive emotions, induced through loving,-kindness meditation, build consequential personal Resources. *Journal of Personality and Social Psychology*, 95(5), 1045-1062. https://www.ncbi.nlm.nih.gov/pmc/articles/PMC3156028/

10. Isen, A. M. (2001). An influence of positive affect on decision making in complex situations: Theoretical issues with practical implications, *Journal of Consumer Psychology*, 11(2), 75-85.

11. Leaf, C. (2021). *Cleaning up your mental mess.*, Baker Books, 28.

12. Kross, E. (2021). *Chatter*, Vermilion, 161-165.

13. Morris, B. J. & Zentall, S. R. (2014, August 27). High fives motivate: The effects of gestural and ambiguous verbal praise on motivation. *Frontiers in Psychology*, 5(928). https://doi.org/10.3389/fpsyg.2014.00928

14. Barrett, L. F. (2020). *7 ½ lessons about the brain.* Houghton Mifflin Harcourt, 88-89.

15. Walsh, M. (2018, February). Their breakthrough formula: Women CEOs. *Korn Ferry Briefing Magazine.* https:// www.kornferry.com/institute/the-breakthrough-formula-women-ceos

16. Seligman, M. E. P., Steen, T. A., Park, N., & Peterson, C. (2005). Positive psychology progress: Empirical validation of interventions. *American Psychologist*, 60(5), 410–421. https://doi.org/10.1037/0003-066X.60.5.410

17. Kini, P., Wong, J., McInnis, S., Gabana, N., & Brown, J. W. (2016). The effects of gratitude expression on neural activity. *Neuro-Image*, 138,1-10.

Chapter 4: Growth

1. https://www.upi.com/Odd_News/2021/11/11/physics-phd-89-years-old-Brown-University/7621636665251/

2. https://www.renaissance.com/edwords/growth-mindset/

3. https://www.fastcompany.com/40457458/satya-nadella-rewrites-microsofts-code

4. Zes, D. & Landis, D. (2013, August). A better return on self-awareness: Companies with higher rates of return on stock also have employees with few personal blind spots. Proof Point, *Korn/Ferry Institute*.

5. David, S. (2016, September 6). You can write your way out of an emotional funk. Here's how. *The Cut*. https://www.thecut.com/2016/09/journaling-can-help-you-out-of-a-bad-mood.html

6. https://centerforbrainhealth.org/article/protect-brain-life-follow-expert-strategies

7. Seijts, G. H. & Latham, G. P. (2005, February). The Academy of Management Executive (1993-2005). *Academy of Management*, 19 (1),124-131 http://www.jstor.org/stable/4166157

8. https://youtu.be/N2QZM7azGoA

9. https://www.apa.org/monitor/2016/11/growth-trauma#:~:text=Post%2Dtraumatic%20growth%20(PTG),often%20see%20positive%20growth%20afterward

Chapter 5: Clarify

1. Cindy Lewis, CEO AirBorn, personal interview, May 19, 2010.

2. Franklin, B., Rogers, G. L. (editor) & Hamer, J. (illustrator), (1996, June 1). The art of virtue: His formula for successful living. *Acorn Publishing*, 3rd edition.

3. Daniel Jones, CEO, Encore Wire, personal interview, Feb. 20, 2022.

Chapter 6: Connect

1. https://www.fords.org/blog/post/from-life-changing-to-world-changing-keeping-the-spirit-of-come-from-away-alive/

2. Jehn, K. A. & Shah, P. P. (1997). Interpersonal relationships and task performance: An examination of mediating processes in friendship and acquaintance groups. *Journal of Personality and Social Psychology, 72*(4), 775-790.

3. Schnall, S., Harper, K. D., Stefanucci, J. K., & Proffitt, D. R. (2008). Social support and the perception of geographical slant. *Journal of Experimental Social Psychology, 44*,1246-1255. Doi:10.1016/j.jesp.2008.04.011

4. Rath, T. & Clifton, D.O. (2004). *How full is your bucket?* New York: Gallup.

5. Greg Brown, senior vice president and chief customer service officer, Blue Cross Blue Shield, personal interview, Feb. 21, 2022.

Chapter 7: Coach

1. Triplett, N. (1898). The dynamogenic factors in pacemaking and competition. *The American Journal of Psychology 9, 4*, 507-533. http://dx.doi.org/10.2307/1412188

2. Bregman P. & Jacobson, H. (2021, September 22). *You can change other people.* Wiley, 1st edition.

3. Darren Woodson, partner, esrp, personal interview, Oct. 21, 2021.

4. https://www.cnbc.com/2018/07/23/3-lasting-lessons-from-jim-rohn-the-man-who-mentored-tony-robbins.html

5. https://www.businessinsider.com/tony-robbins-changed-his-life-at-17-years-old-2017-10

6. Corporate Leadership Council (2002). Building the high potential workforce: A quantitative analysis of the effectiveness of performance management strategies, *Corporate Executive Board*. 29-30.

7. Andrew Levi, CEO, PlantTAGG, personal interview, June 12, 2018.

8. https://financiallysimple.com/worlds-best-ceo-winner-jeff-immelt-shares-his-list-of-leadership-must-dos/

9. https://www.cnbc.com/2022/01/04/toyota-dethrones-gm-to-become-americas-top-selling-automaker-in-2021.html

Acknowledgments

We know well that nothing in life is achieved alone, so we extend our heartfelt thanks and deep gratitude to those whose hearts and minds are reflected in this book.

We praise God for providing the opportunities for us to learn and grow, and then to equip and encourage leaders with our insights. We are extremely grateful that He has brought the following people into our lives:

Our three children—for helping us expand our capacity for love and hone our leadership practices on the home front.

Friends and colleagues—for generously gifting us their valuable time and feedback.

Clients—for partnering with us to test and refine our various leadership models over the years, including the *Healthy Leadership* principles and practices.

David Cottrell, CEO of CornerStone Leadership Institute—for being a steadfast and trusted friend, mentor, co-author, business partner, and publisher since our first book in 2003.

Aaron Schulman—for providing clear thinking to help realize our vision for this book.

Deb Johnson—for her expert editing and hyper-speed responsiveness to elevate the quality of this book.

Melissa Farr—for always being a delight to work with, and for designing this book cover and interior on our 13th project together.

Kathleen Green Pothier—for her keen eye and detailed proofing.

You, the reader—for choosing to invest in yourself and your team.

Reinforcement Resources

1. Healthy Leadership Checkup
Free three-minute, online self-assessment with a real-time feedback report here:

theLgroup.com/healthy-leadership-checkup

2. Keynote Presentation
Invite the authors to deliver an upbeat, engaging message to encourage and motivate your leaders.

3. Training
Equip your organization's leaders with actionable tools to cultivate healthy leadership.

4. Executive Coaching
The Executive Navigation[SM] coaching process is results-focused and supported by field-tested tools to help you elevate your leadership. Clients measurably and significantly improve personal productivity and team performance.

5. Complimentary Insights and Encouragement
Text "leadership" to 833-250-7377 to receive insights and encouragement for healthy leadership directly to your inbox.

THE **L** GROUP

Leadership Advisors | dedicated to healthy growth

Strategy　　Coaching　　Speaking　　Resources　　Training

214.789.8053 • theLgroup.com

About the Authors

Lee J. Colan, Ph.D., is an organizational psychologist and CEO advisor. He applies an in-depth understanding of business, science, people, and organizations to help leaders and organizations grow. As a result, he quickly helps leaders bring order where there is chaos, clarity where there is ambiguity, and growth where there is decline.

He has written and co-authored fifteen popular leadership books that have been translated into ten languages, including the best-selling *Engaging the Hearts and Minds of All Your Employees* and *Sticking to It: The Art of Adherence.*

Lee earned his doctorate in Organizational Psychology from George Washington University after graduating from Florida State University.

Julie Davis-Colan, M.S. is a CEO advisor and corporate health strategist. She applies a powerful combination of brain science, positive psychology, and perspective-changing insights. Julie keenly observes and deeply listens. This enables her to see and hear the unrecognized truths in others revealing gifts and capabilities that open a new world of opportunity and growth.

She has co-authored seven popular books, including *Orchestrating Attitude* and *The Power of Positive Coaching.*

Julie earned her master's degree in Preventive Medicine from The Ohio State University's College of Medicine after graduating from Florida State University. She is also one of 1,400 people worldwide certified as a Positive Psychology Practitioner by The Flourishing Center.

theLgroup.com

Healthy Leadership

Help your team and your business thrive!

Available at **CornerStoneLeadership.com** and Amazon.

These quantity discounts available
at **CornerStoneLeadership.com**:

1-10 copies	$19.95
11-50 copies	$17.95
51+ copies	$15.95